Tan Raptures

Tan Raptures

Alan Morrison

Smoke Stack Books

Smokestack Books
1 Lake Terrace, Grewelthorpe, Ripon HG4 3BU
e-mail: info@smokestack-books.co.uk
www.smokestack-books.co.uk

Text copyright 2017,
Alan Morrison, all rights reserved.

ISBN 978-0-9955635-0-6

Smokestack Books is
represented by Inpress Ltd

*This book is dedicated
to the memories
of over 91,000 victims
of Tory 'welfare reform'*

Contents

Green Tinder
Digger Hinges	13
The Moving Rainbow	16
Down the Rainbow Sliding	21
Olvido Verde – Olives Bleed Green	23
Red Generals	39
The Abandoned Shade	40
Greeks Bearing Rifts	41
The Green Heart of Germany	50

Red Wilderness
When is a Red Swede a Beetroot?	55
Where's Wal?	56
Thaxted Redux	57
Cuttslowe Walls	62
Wootton Bassett	63
Red Flag to a Bulldog	65
Taser Dawn	67
Ash Friday	69

Coventry Blue
Thatcher's Statue	73
Glossolalia	75
Reading George Orwell's review of *Mein Kampf* at Liverpool Lime Street Station	84
Orwell Mansions	90
New Era	93
Eton Mess	95
Coventry Blue	99

Tan Raptures
The Decision Makers: A Coventry Story 117
The Bedroom Taxidermy 124
The Significs of Gentrification 126
The Disinfecting Sunlight 129
Going Dutch 138
Auld Reekie's Black Spot 140
Clapson's Cap 142
Tan Raptures 145

Notes 183

**Green
Tinder**

Digger Hinges

for the Runnymede Diggers 2012

Squatters of the grasslands over the river from Runnymede
Where John Lackland scratched his mark on Magna Carta, 1215/
2012: youth of England lack any land, while boundaries

Are in abundance, patchworks multiply, cramp up sympathy;
On damp campus water meadows stove-lights glow in Surrey,
Children of the forest sell-offs, berried Gerrard Winstanleys,

Camouflage caps for capotains, blacks, brackens, khakis
Patched in disruptive patterns – Diggers in Greenleaf fatigues;
Lilburne's cherubs rigged in sea-green ribbons, sprigs of rosemary,

Offspring of empty purse-strings, a borrowed rainbow army
Simmering a common broth from beetroots, sprouts and poetry,
Pamphleteering butterflies primed in leaf-mimic liveries

Reciting seventeenth century verses blotching under eaves
Of dripping twigs; moss-roofed refuseniks with capped knees,
Cropped of hope and property; renters of sheltering leaves

Carving woodchipped bed-sits out from hollowed loins of trees;
No re-enactments needed in parchment-catching histories
Of Cobham, Wellingborough and Iver (Bucks) communities:

Commonweal clamped, Welfare State Turned Upside Down by Tories'
Torching of social tenancies, drubs of verboten poverties –
Dole books now taboo as Latin Bibles of priest-holed popery

Hollow-knocked by Roundheads, no giro says boo to a goosey;
No sanctuary in countryside for homeless of Home Counties,
Barely an acre of hill or scrubland un-inscribed by absentee

Landlords' stinging signs: *NO TRESPASSING! PRIVATE PROPERTY!*
NIMBYs tramp their tents and crops, re-evict city evictees –
Generation Tent turfed out from gentrified streets and trees,

Expelled as social lepers, purged to umbrageous canopies;
Thumpers of upturned bathtubs charged on top-up empties,
Mocked as dreadlocked drop-outs, *'Trustafarians', 'Crusties'*;

A Hunting of the Boxes backdrops Bobbies' *'selfies'*:
Porcine snapshots' damp protestor spoils displayed as trophies;
Locked in cells with hefty fines – but hearts are locket territories

Scallop-clasped to grasping hands; sempiternal properties:
Spirits outstrip fleecing rents of bodies' shorthold tenancies…

Long grasses of sprung ideas, greening wounds on dungarees,
Pitched hopes can't be uprooted like poles of pop-up tepees,
Nor can brass mottos be obscured by bruise-blue verdigris:

'To make the waste lands grow' gongs an age old pedigree
Of singed egalitarianism spiralling in perigees
Through Anglo-Saxon Golden Ages ringing in the genes

And rinsing through the guts of Englishness, centuries'
Woodcut rhetoric, Communist Dendrochronology,
Tree-ring radicalism, green-bough pledge of grass lessees

Brokered by young Brackenborough, knowledge by dug degrees
(Ripe scholarship rusticating outside Brunel's faculties),
Sore-thumb Rainsborough boxed in Facebook redoubts, Twitter feeds;

Utopian pilot, as all past figureheads of his sea-green breed,
Agitators thrust up from pitched pulpits of Hedge Priests;
English Progress swings on Digger hinges and anti-rusting grease;

Giro Goodgroomes, Virtual Everards and Wireless Winstanleys
Occupy the open spaces of non-partitioned Memories,
No patchworks sprawl on maps of strip system topographies;

Blogging Diggers, wireless Levellers, plough fields, threads, sow seeds
Of fellowship in hearts and minds, through laptop posting sprees;
Raise crops in common ownership of Javascript Countries;

Spread broadsides on grapevines from greengages and Blackberries;
Blues and Purples, natural English tinges, yet Reds and Greens
Have been here digging rainbows since the seventeenth century;

Watermelons were imported into England, 1615,
But only when Green rinds are crushed are their Red insides seen…

O English Progress swings on Digger hinges and anti-rusting grease…

The Moving Rainbow

1

Spark up your Lucifers and spare a thought
For the phossy-jawed matchgirls who struck a match
Back in 1888, which would conflagrate and catch
Across the sulphur-clouded working classes
And ultimately thwart the callous factory owners
At *Bryant & May* from keeping matchstick workers
On crippling pay, their diminutive frames shrunk
More with malnourishment, and metabolisms
Slowly poisoned with daily exposure to fumes
Of toxic white phosphorous used to coat the tips
Of matchsticks to make them combustible –
Sesquisulfide formula of unforeseen side-effects,
Disfigurements, the only usufruct fruits they'd pick:
Slowly rotting jawbones to the overpowering stench
Of rancid abscesses, fungal gums, mouths and necks
Scaled and swollen – mermaids of the lymph nodes
Marooned from Celtic Twilights – as if from scrofula
Or some stunted protean syndrome, piscine as
Opposed to elephantine as in the case of capped-
And-hooded Joseph Merrick, rescued from the gas-lit
Freak shows, and, in that same spark-struck year,
Confined to the boiler-clanging attic of London
Hospital under the care of Dr Frederick Treves,
Where this *'elephant man'* spent his seclusion
Painstakingly constructing accurate scale models
Of London landmarks out of card and matchsticks…

2

No canons manufactured by Bofors would have fired
Salutes to such murderous industriousness
Countenanced by Savile Row-suited, cigar-toting
Bosses of the British Lucifer trade; and hatching
Capitalists at *Swedish Match* would have scorned such
Daily manslaughter in the cause of cutting costs
To puff up profits, that wasn't the Scandinavian
Way – although *Bryant & May* had traded in Swedish-
Imported matches since 1850 – and was snatched
Up by the mighty Stockholm manufacturer in
1927, *Swedish Match* having stalked to high stakes
Since Ivar Kreuger started up the firm in Jönköping
('*City of matches*') back in 1917... The matchgirls'
Struggle gained support from middle-class hatchling
Activists: Clementina Black (a kind of British avatar
Of Kata Dalström, Sweden's outspoken social agitator
And Christian-Communist) helped organise them,
While theosophist and fellow socialist bluestocking,
Annie Besant, was a sympathetic campaigner for
Their cause, spoke up in public on these London-Irish
Lasses' scandalous working conditions, spun polemic
Championing their plight in her halfpenny weekly,
The Link; also a novice clairvoyant whose ear alone
Had captured Madame Blavatsky's last whispered wish:
'*Don't leave the link unbroken*' – cryptic, uncanny request
From a violet-eyed chain-smoking Russian spirit-
Medium who could conjure up pennies from the rustling
Depths of her tobacco pouch, if she felt the pinch...

3

But the matchstick girls were spirited enough to take
Upon themselves the grit of their indigence, throw
Caution and matches to catch on the winds, risk
Losing bone-crippling livelihoods to protest, campaign
And picket outside *Bryant & May's* clattering factory
Gates in Bow, every day, after shifts, apparelled
Uproariously in wide hats with giant feathers of vivid
Colours shouting over tiny heads with short-trimmed hair
Surmounting gaunt angular visages – more austere
Proto-flappers – marching defiantly in high-heeled
Boots, strutting peacocks shocking passers by,
Perceived as bolshie harlots from the land of bogs
And barnacles, but no self-disrespecting strumpets
Blew such loud sartorial trumpets in broad daylight
As they who were avoided like the clap, or the plague
That stank out their mouths with fetor – leprous
Leprechaunesses; and when they tromped together
Onto Westminster, a troop of shrunken suffragettes
Without a match between them, some described the sight
As if witnessing a rainbow moving towards them,
For the feathers of red, orange, yellow, green, blue,
Indigo and violet – such a sight as theirs had not been
Witnessed in Bow since the seventeenth century,
With the hair-cropped prospect of lace-collared Levellers'
Wives carrying bunches of rosemary behind
Husbands shaded in broad-brimmed black felt hats
Plumed with its sprigs, coats tagged with sea-green ribbons,
Brides and grooms of the Rosemary Branch, Islington;
Those Irish Sulphuresses flashing white, green, violet –
Prophetic colours of future Suffragettes, better-
Heeled inheritors of these class-obscured harbingers…

4

The feisty Irish matchgirls brandished hatpins at would-
Be assailants, prepared to prick at Peelers who might
Try to arrest them; and, in the end, these miniature
Women, phosphorous blossoms, caused such a public
Spectacle, impressing Parliament with their sharpness
And eloquence in putting their case, that *Bryant &
May* was embarrassed into agreeing their terms:
That they'd receive a fairer wage, be better protected
In future from the acrid fumes used for coating Lucifers,
And would no longer be deemed as of lesser value
Than the machinery they operated, machinery
Which frequently sliced off their thumbs and fingers –
Once seen as affordable sacrifices, collateral damage,
Expendable appendages, a cinch for loss adjusters –
And resulted in instant dismissal sans severance pay
Or compensation, as the factory bosses massaged digits,
Docked the matchgirls' wages for '*offences*' such as '*talking*',
'*Going to the toilet*' or '*dropping matches*'; nor would
The abscessed casualties be any longer left to quietly
Rot away in dingy corners of the factory floor – and more:
By 1906, the Berne Convention debuted, a belated
Treaty negotiated in Switzerland, prohibiting white or
Yellow phosphorous in match production… But those
Sparking matchstick girls gained more than simply
Their own less hazardous working conditions and
The setting up of a contrapuntal union: they sparked up
A trail of fireworks across the working classes, fizzing,
Howling, blazing displays of protest that ricocheted,
Inspiring the London Dockers then other trades to form
Themselves into unions to petition and campaign
For better work conditions and a liveable wage,
For the dignity they always say comes automatically
Through labour, its' inalienable contract, more than just
An expedient capitalist pact, but a mutual Covenant
Through which risk and responsibility go both ways,
In cooperative exchange, not simply in the bosses' interests,
The interminable chain between manager, shop steward
And dogsbody, Master, go-between and wage-Slave…

5

Remember, remember 1888, when *Bryant & May's*
Striking matchstick workers struck a light for an end
To industrial slavery, and hold still firm today
As our torch-tipped Tory Captains *'Make Work Pay'*
In every way but through a wage: in indignity
And ever-depleting rights, scrapping Health and Safety
Protections, euphemised as *'slashing red tape'* and
'Making it easier to employ (exploit) more people',
Using Aunt Sallies of *'fiscal consolidation'* and *'balancing
The books'* (in the bosses' favour, of course), turning
The clocks back to manslaughter days of iniquitous
Factories, malicious workhouses, boneless unions,
'Zero-hours contracts', dismantling the Welfare State,
Airbrushing it out of history, as if it had never been
Struck up in the first place… Remember the matchgirls
Of *Bryant & May* – lustrous blooms of *'moving rainbow'*:
For those *Rare Young Girls* did not *Battle In Vain*,
But fought for all our rights, so long taken for granted,
And for a better settlement of employment; nettles
Prickling their veins *Blossomed Into Victory* against
The bosses for *Rights* and *Gains* now endangered again:
Over a century later, their legacy regains urgency
In a long oncoming night that threatens newborn pains,
Babes of labour tipped out with bathwaters into brimstone
Flames, the matchgirls' cause almost forgotten,
Along with sulphur stains, but not so *Bryant & May's,*
Their brand rattles on – under mother-firm *Swedish
Match* – and its matches scrape red phosphorous to spark
Up flames, and cash-strapped, blacklisted picketers
Must once more strike a light against intransigent grains
Of industrial night, and wait for the spark to catch again…

Down the Rainbow Sliding

> *'Touching with your long fingers a marble lyre. …*
> *A winged Idea down the rainbow sliding, …*
> *All ranks you visit, courteous swamp-foul.*
> *The world's great engines pound asthmatically …*
> *Man walks to man across a trembling swamp.*
> *The scientific sportsman lifts his gun …*
> *And you fall spluttering, a specific bird.*
> *I see your stuffed breast and boot-button eyes …*
> *And lean on my umbrella thoughtfully…'*
> Christopher Caudwell, *Hymn to Philosophy (1937)*

Christopher St. John Sprigg ('St. John' singed to 'Sindgen')
Hailed from 53 Montserrat Road, Putney, raised by
Roman Catholics, schooled at Ealing Priory under strict
Instruction of Benedictines – left at fifteen when his father,
Stanhope, lost his job as literary editor at the *Daily Express*;
The teenage son cut his teeth as a reporter on the *Yorkshire
Observer*, shadow-padre in tow, as he took up his Bradford post;
Prompt at one score and seven, Christopher was struck by
His *Das Kapital* Damascus moment – Karl Marx and Friedrich
Engels, his Hegelian guides; by 1934, Comrade Sprigg
Registered membership with the Poplar Communist Party;

Switched his surname to the pseudonymous 'Caudwell' for
The works that would stamp his posthumous mark, no mere

Journalism, but polemical monographs and treatises
On philosophy, poetry, politics, physics – all the p-s;
Hermeneutics cut from cloth of dialectical materialism,
Nothing and no one escaped the scalpels of his precocious

Scholarship; all of his works – bar books on aeronautics –
Posthumously published: the pioneering *Illusion and
Reality, Studies in a Dying Culture, The Crisis
In Physics; Poems*… December '36, same time as Jason
Gurney, he volunteered for Spain's Republic, trained as a machine-
Gunner, International Brigades, at Albecete… Jarama

Claimed him, when his Charcot light machine-gun jammed whilst
Aimed at hurtling Moors raining hails of hand-grenades
Under cover of Fascist artillery and planes; valiantly manning
Defences with Clem Beckett till the last of the retreat fell back –
Wintringham (wounded), Sinfield, Rust survived as witnesses to
Events: the dug-in gunners' courage shielding them with rattling
Laughter of metallic catarrh… Caudwell's shadow ebbed to red,
Laid down the rainbow sliding, galley proofs left uncorrected…

Olvido Verde – Olives Bleed Green

1

The Oxford Reds changed their suits and brogues
For olive berets and brown togs of corduroyed Brigades,
Or white tunics of ambulance men, scrambled up
The parapets of Spain as soon as the vacancy came up
For its Republic to be reoccupied before the pincer-
Movement of a prowling Fascist coup pounced in to fill it:
Carlists and Falangists, a new vanguard of Visigoths
And Vorticists – and so soon, only five years since
The Republic's difficult birth, from an avalanching
Vote in the first democratic election since smouldering
Ember days of Don Miguel Primo de Rivera y
Orbaneja, 2nd Marquis of Estella, 22nd Count
Of Sobremonte, Knight of Calatrava – who seized power
As dictator in 1923, overthrown by King Alfonso
Seven years later (caricatured as Rivera's *'dancing
Partner'*), who then went into chronic exile… But by
Summer '36, the Falange (the Spanish Phalanx),
Formed by Rivera's son Don José Antonio Primo de
Rivera y Sáenz de Heredia – 1st Duke of Primo de
Rivera, 3rd Marquis of Estella, Grandee of Spain –
Marched against the people's democratic government…

2

This impasse at the cusp of partisan confrontation,
A Visigoth Ragnarök of Gods and Giants,
An historic Hispanic clash of Titans Left and Right,
About to be played out in panoramic scope on tan
Spanish pastures, depicted as a new crusade by both
Sides of the armed dispute: not only Carlists and Falangists
Had waited in the wings for a chance to recapture Spain
From the ascendant peasant classes so that the aristocrats
And land-owners could put them back to the pitchfork
And plough by the whip-hand – but many young left-wing
European progressives longed for an honourable cause
For which to sacrifice unfocused, smoky, bookish lifestyles,
In the names of freedom, democracy and, for many,
Socialism – as Robin Skelton pinpointed in *Poetry
Of the Thirties* nearly thirty years later: '*The Spanish Civil
War usefully combined both obsessions of the rootless
Left-wing thinkers of the time, 'community' and 'war'* –
Skelton expanded on his anatomy of the pathology
Of the Thirties Generation in relation to this psychical
Spanish Wash: '*…the rebellion of the generals could be
Seen as the attack of reactionary capitalism
Upon progressive socialism. The Spanish Civil War was
A symbol become reality*' (and more than just a metaphor
To Christopher Caudwell); '*It embodied the class struggle,
And also the struggle of the artists against the philistines
(Did not the Fascists murder Lorca? Was not Picasso
On the side of the Government?)*' (though not so Dalí
And Pound!)… '*The Spanish War… caught the poets' imaginations*'
(Those '*fire-eaters*', as seasonal correspondent Cyril
Connolly branded them); '*Many joined the International
Brigade. It seemed* de rigueur *to visit Spain, and to lend
One's name, if not always one's armed presence, to the cause
Of the workers*'; Auden and Spender both conducted tours,
'*The former as a stretcher bearer, the latter as head of English
Broadcasting in a radio station … found to be defunct*'…
Only mad dogs and Englishmen go out in the Madrid sun…

3

An unprecedented splash of poets and assorted men
Of letters put aside their pens for weapons in defence
Of Spanish democracy: Communist poets conscripted
By their consciences, red verse volunteers: Auden, Spender,
Wintringham, Orwell (in a fetching chocolate balaclava);
Anglo-Hungarian journalist, Arthur Koestler, captured by
The Francoists, denounced as a Communist agent provocateur,
And put under sentence of death, but, exchanged for
A high profile Nationalist prisoner – so survived
To write his *Dialogue with Death*, and *Spanish Testament*
(A Left Book Club Choice from Victor Gollancz with
An ermined Introduction from the Duchess of Atholl) –
Koestler would exit strictly at a time of his own choosing,
After a prolific book list, and first marks of leukaemia
And Parkinsonism – his departing note recapturing
That *'oceanic feeling'* that had crept peacefully over him
At times of greatest peril, and found him anticipating
'A de-personalised after-life beyond due confines of space,
Time and matter and beyond the limits of our comprehension…';
And those ripe green promises whose posterities were
Already inscribed in Spanish lead, philosopher-soldiers
But of a very different stripe to the blond Wagnerians
Their fathers had aimed at from Belgium's muddier dugouts;
Julian Bell's blood spilt to bruise the Bloomsbury set;
Irish Left Republican, Charles Donnelly, sliced by
Gunfire as he broke cover from behind an olive tree,
Last sighted squeezing olives in his hands while muttering
'Even the olives are bleeding' – O olives bleed green,
So too those bleeding green olives of khaki plucked ripe
From the branches to which they transplanted themselves
From foggy English groves and misty Irish shires:
Rupert John Cornford, a perfect target standing up
In the suntrap of his head-bandage, picked off by snipers
The day after his 21st birthday; Christopher St. John
Sprigg (aka Caudwell), Marxist polemicist-cum-poet,
Difficult cousin of Audenic dialectic, taken out
Somewhere between illusion and reality, still wet behind
The ears, Spanish with tears, eucalyptus tears; scents

Of saffron, cinnamon and oranges wafting in the thick
Moroccan balm of the dusty gardened square in Granada
Under the vertiginous Moorish glare of the Al Hambra's
Camouflaged Islamic damask interior (its' dizzying
Indoor decorations spiked with hyperkulturemia);
Near the sign pointing to the Manuel de Falla Auditorium;
And outdoor cafés where light-fingered gypsies throng
With boot brushes, lift foreign ankles onto foot-boxes
Without permissions, tourists at first thinking the coffee
Is taking the weight off their feet: unsponsored shoe
Polishing for the price of *pan y vino*; where tomb-bruised
Tobacconists tout sun-scorched chiaroscuro postcards
Of folkloric Lorca, homosexual, Communist and poet –
A triple-target for *la fascista*, sacrificial Faun trampled
Under stampedes of cloven-hoofed Centaurs' *encierro*…

4

Spain is so heavy, wine-heavy, vividly liverish,
Particularly in long-enslaved Andalusia
Under yokes of lictors, melting pot of extremes
Its peasant farmers had no means to repel – crushed
And consumed by Franco's coup as easily as a roasted
Canary's skull; since the fascists' victory, struck dumb by
The aftershock of Francoism, the long pounding hangover
Of the Censorship when opposing opinions and poetries
Had to seep out silently through pores of sweatshop
Populaces oppressed by polished booted populism,
Policed by the Guardia Civil, Spanish Gendarmerie,
Originally deployed to suppress revolutionary
Predilections in rural quarters, retard the spread of anti-
Monarchism – uniformed bullies mobilised on behalf
Of the Bourbons to intimidate the mobs, sharply attired
In moss-coloured tunics, scalps cropped by quadrangular
Back-to-front *tricornio* of shiny patent leather, angular
Liquorice hats like crumpled umbrellas, so feared and
Respected, rumours spread these gleaming black symmetrical
Beetles invested violence in the wearers, as if by sorcery,
Hexes, bewitching enchantments, as in 'El Amor Brujo'
From de Falla's *Three-Cornered Hat* – taut violin-strings
Reverberating buzzing bees, droning angry stings…

5

Spain has never known plain-sailing, has ever been thrown
Off course into choppier waters by its sun-struck sons
And daughters, but its intensity is infectious, driven
With an avid vitalism that charges the blood – '*You will
Feel you are alive out there*' waxed a young David Gascoyne
When contrasting war-struck Spain with Thirties British
Retailed acedia, commodity-fetishism in the midst
Of economic Depression: '*Here everything is so unreal*...;
John Boulting's correspondence with Marjorie Battcock
From Hampstead Peace Council decried the Eliotic
Landscape of London as '*dirty, disorder and terrifying din…
A fitting accompaniment*'; stone-faced workers from
Abertillery standing to attention by their placards
In support of the shrapnel-splintered Spanish Republic, captured
In a photograph with steel-spirited Dolores Ibárruri,
'*La Pasionaria*', champion of the poor and oppressed,
Who paraphrased Zapata: '*Better to die on your feet, than live
On your knees*'; and was the first person to shout '*!No Pasarán!*'
('*They shall not pass*') at the approaching fascist war-machine…
'*Spain Days*' splashed colour in British cities, foggy fiestas
Sporting kiosks selling Republican flags of red, purple
And yellow, brochures, pamphlets and ephemera in support
Of the Popular Front – some composed by Catholic Socialists,
Such as Monica Whately, who refused to be acquiescent
To the Francoists simply because some rogue Loyalists
Had shot a few priests: because Democracy's crusaders
Were their comrades of a truer Sacred Heart; and Spanish
Shops popped up all over the place – one in Southwark –
Promoting Spain's Republican cause; four thousand British
Volunteers to the International Brigades and POUM
(Partido Obrero de Unificación Marxista), comprising,
Among others, the Garibaldi Brigade, the Abraham Lincoln
Brigade (summoning to mind platoons in black stovepipes
And chin curtains), the Major Attlee Battalion, the Dimitrov
Battalion, et al, to face the hordes of Franco's Spanish
Foreign Legion and formidable turbaned Moors – Davids, all,
Against Goliaths of tanks and Messerschmitts – '*¡No
Pasarán!...*' But the fascists passed into future history…

6

Fascism was –and always is – the ultimately volcanic
Build-up of malcontents' catarrh in the rasping
Capitalist trachea, the bile churned up by the friction
Between poverty and competition, abrasive
Vibrations harvested by divisions of Haves, Have-Nots,
Will-Haves and Grabs-By-Any-Means, resentments
Against conspicuous consumption amidst pecuniary
Amputation, penury in propinquity to plenty,
Elastic as hatred, strung from chronic insecurity,
Neurosis, fear, anger, unhinged greed, rampant grasping,
Animal spirits, dog-eat-dog, throwing out dead wood,
Law of the jungle and survival of the fittest –
The common roods – augmented by material
Brutality and acquisitive behaviours; fascism was
'...*according to the dialectical analysis of Marxism…*
The expression of capitalism in its death throes. Faced
With the growth of labour organizations and… working-
Class demands for social reform, capitalism was preparing
To abandon even the forms of liberal democracy
Which had served it well enough hitherto, and was falling
Back upon open reaction and violence to oppress
The proletariat' – so argued historian David Thomson
In *Europe Since Napoleon*; '*It sought to divert popular*
Attention toward national aggrandizement rather than
Improvement of social conditions. The slog-arm bands
Of fascism, the hirelings of the capitalist class, the latest
Instrument of that war …inherent in bourgeois society…'

7

In response to the rise of the Far Right back then, Fabian
Pacifists and graduates of gradualism – G.D.H. Cole
Among them – campaigned for a *'British People's Front'* against
Fascism, but even the Labour Party wouldn't take up
This campaign; so tensions boiled over on the Continent,
*'Communism and fascism tended… to be twin barometers
Rising and falling together'*, and when both barometers
Matched in momentum, all chaos broke out, and the first
Nation to be tipped into chronic confrontation, Civil
War, was Spain, the first example of the reality-rupture
Wrought by opposite wings: *Spain*: proleptic amphitheatre
Of war, of a stand staged against the armoured march
Of fascism… The *Daily Worker* was more prescient than
Its press competitors (as it still is today under the banner
Of the *Morning Star* – or, by subscribers' sobriquet, 'the *Daily
Miracle*'): in '33 its' first-ever women's page scooped some
Choicest items, ostensibly on high fashion with a dose
Of sardonic comparisons (only the *Daily Worker* could
Politicise the sartorial), one piece on the expulsion
Of a Communist from the Co-op Women's Guild which
Contrasted diamonds and gowns adorning that season's
Debutantes with items on miners' wives and women
Factory workers, while also reporting on a female
Spanish militant who'd been imprisoned for a *'monstrous'*
Twenty-five years; struggles of senoras and senoritas
Were being depicted in that socialist paper a whole three years
Before Franco's coup ripped apart the People's ripe Republic…

8

1937 – bouleversement – the *Left Review* (founded by
Tom Wintringham, Commander of the Major Attlee Battalion,
International Brigade), conducted a survey under Nancy
Cunard's signature, asking all thinkers, conscientious
Projectors, vintage cognoscenti of the age, to tick whether
They supported Republican Spain, or the fascist uprising –
Titled '*The Question*', the census pitched itself firmly in
Nordic-green 'Auden Country' with a spirited call to arms:
'*The equivocal attitude, the Ivory Tower, the paradoxical,*
The ironic detachment, will no longer do' (O who is there
To say this *TODAY? Who?*); prune-faced Samuel Beckett sent
In his answer on a postcard in one schizophasic splurge
With appropriately Hispanic punctuation: '*¡UPTHEREPUBLIC!*'
O that totemic upside-down Spanish exclamation mark!
Vital though it was not to romanticise the more progressive
Side in this upcoming conflict, it was paramount to support
The apparatus of a compassionate Republic – true,
There were atrocities committed in both wind directions:
'*The moderate Republican Government of the consumptive*
Casares Quiroga was weak and harassed from both sides.
The tactics of the Falangists and extreme Left alike were
Those of terrorism and violence', but it was the Right
That was the most brutal, particularly the Falangists,
Who even attacked their cousin activists '*with rotten eggs,*
Insults, and broken windows', as well as socialists and
Communists '*with personal terrorism and murder*', and
'*Judges who condemned Falangists to prison, or journalists*
Who attacked them in the press, were assassinated', they gave
No inch to anyone who outflanked them and their comrades-
In-arms: '*In Madrid cars of* escuadristas *went round the streets,*
Armed with machine guns, shooting down …political enemies' –
Like some marauding limousine-and-magazined Mafia;
While some extremists of the Left were rumoured to
Have hunted down men of the cloth, many of whom
Were suspected as agents provocateurs in surplices,
Collaborators with Carlists and Falangists; '*The anarchists*
And communists resorted to lightning strikes and shooting affrays'…

9

All in all, *'economic depression and poor harvests wove*
A backcloth of unemployment and hunger, completing all
The conditions favourable to civil war' – which finally
Ruptured and avalanched after the assassination
Of the pre-Republic dictatorship's former Minister
Of Finance, Calvo Sotelo, on 13 July 1936, thereafter
'The military junta headed by General Sanjurjo, led an army
Revolt in the Spanish zone of Morocco and on 16th July
Occupied Ceuta and Melilla… The next day the officers
Of the garrisons rose in almost every city in Spain. Sanjurjo
Was killed in a plane accident and his place taken up by
General Francisco Franco' who rallied his Moorish hordes
From the Canaries on 17 and 18 July – thus was
The Falangist flag raised, galloping in the choppy island
Breeze, marking the outbreak of civil hostilities: '*It was,*
In essence, a revolt of the army and the Falangists against
The programme of the Popular Front', the opposite barometer
To fascism, which rose in contradistinction wherever
That brutal, slant-palmed Roman-style salute was raised…
The fascists stomped to triumph, pitched in for the long-
Run and the Censorship – and, today, the kleptocratic
Fist of the Falange-like Troika claws at parched Spain
Laid waste by capitalist austerity – *yet again*: the screaming
Tears of Los Indignados (The Outraged Multitude),
In Madrid and all across the scorched country of dust
And blood and clattering tumbrels of asset-stripped industry,
Lost to the white night of fiscal retrenchment, columns
Of Indignants marching in hats, sticks in hands, all the way
From the Basque Country and the wine-skin pastures
Of Andalusia, striking miners firing makeshift bazookas
At blacklegged police – industrial impasse conflagrates fast
In the incendiary heat of this nation of heavy memories,
Now weighing heavier than ever, catching winds of change…

10

In Hornachuelos, casualised brigades of young
Unemployed Southern Spaniards organise themselves
Into an Andalusian Union of Workers, sequester
The estate of Palacio de Moratalla in the absence
Of its landlord, the Duke of Segorbe, and set to work
Growing crops on abandoned tan fields – the earth
Of their heritage – in order to sustain themselves with wheat
To make their own bread – for, in recession, Spanish children
No more come into the world armed with loaves, but empty-
Handed; these Andalusian Diggers, adumbrating
The anarcho-syndicalism piloted so perilously
In those same parched Southern agricultural heartlands
Back in the mid-Thirties, civil confrontations on the rights
To land ownership, which culminated in the reactionary
Coup against the democratic Republic – but according
To one AUW Spokesman, Senore Cañamero:
*'We're not anarchists looking for conflict, but our claims are
Similar to those of the 1930s... because the land is... under
The control now of even fewer people than at that time'* – so
Too in England's damper pastures where a new breed
Of young green English Diggers are digging in their heels
To till the common soil and *'make the waste lands grow'*...

11

But once this capitalist Falange slackens its grip, and this
Gutless, bloodless White Terror of monetarism shrinks
Back into relative quiet of olive alert, before it dissipates,
Will the Troika propose a second Pact of Forgetting
('*El pacto de olvido*' – or *olvido de olivo* – oblivion of olives…)
As that passed after Franco's death? Will the Spanish
Have to forget and forgive all over again? Be expected
To munch lotuses on their Feast of the Race (*Fiesta de la
Raza*)? Better at least than eating lead as many did
At the same celebration on 12 October '37, in the midst
Of the civil war, lead and roses, bread and circuses –
Curious now cut-price English clothes shops and emporiums
Are selling cheap t-shirts of crimson with modernistic
Lettering reading *No Propaganda/Solo la Victoria/
Tocarlas en su propio juego/Major de raza desde 1937*
Streaking across the chest, *Made in Singapore*, possibly by
Exploited Hindu sweatshop labour in ruptured draperies
Buried under rubble, as the collapsed Rana Plaza,
Occupational hazard of the factory floor for absence
Of Health and Safety Law – (that old '*red tape*'…) –
Such vanishing treatment of history would be blatant
Trampling of the past, wiping the historical slate, smudged
Palimpsest of past repeats – Professor J.H. Plumb would be
Metaphorically up in arms, wielding lead-piping on
The retrospective *Cluedo* board: Plumb argued in *Death
Of the Past*, that the past, being the impartial factual account
Of events, was perennially rearranged into what we call
'*History*' – the clue being in '*story*': a more mythological
Narrative superimposed over the bare bones embellished
Depending on allegiances of hegemonies of any given time:
'*History*' is forty per cent fact, eighty per cent propaganda…

12

Not only Spain but all of Europe will be made to forget
The days when democracy itself was up for grabs by
Carpetbaggers, floated for a song on the stock exchange;
When the parasitic markets dictated every nation state's
Fiscal policy; when sovereignties were spilt like coins
Into pockets of plutocrats, while citizens' lives were put
On timocratic tabs and kleptocratic slates – no, Spain
Is too rooted to its past to forget, in spite of best efforts
To construct a new *olvido*, throw back the old Republic's
Rallying cry in the faces of its' disinherited children:
The Past shall not pass! It will be rewritten in numerical
Symbols, numbers, algebra, by deducting – the world is ruled by
Numbers punctuating a clock ticking like a time-bomb
For endangered *demos*: even now, in our so-called
Democracies, our privatised governments are joining up
The dots and realising which side their bread is buttered on –
Desk-service for vested shadow interests over the citizens
They're supposed to represent; democracy can be circum-
-navigated if needs be, corners cut; no one will notice it
Being trimmed down bit by bit through nepotisms and
Peculiar handshakes; and hasty rewrites of recent-past
Statutes through *'retrospective legislations'*, not only can
History be rewritten (even if just to be repeated almost
Verbatim), but democracy can be readjusted to scratch
Despotic itches – it's ever been thus, and there's always
Some useful purpose certain modicums of fascism can
Be put to in the service of democratic freedom – it's just
The difference between softly, softly and less genteel
Persuasion; and who's to object, apart from unsolicited
Poets and protestors? *Us?* There *is* no *Us…* Not since *They*
Gambled it all away – now there's just *You* versus *Me…*

13

In the end, democracy will be packed up in a carpet bag
Along with all those other thoroughly good-egg ideas –
Christianity, republicanism, Communism, Socialism,
And so on – sadly all of which withered away in the end
Like potted aspidistras in damp gloom-plunged avocado-
Coloured hallways of mildewed English terraces,
In spite of the best efforts of spinsters to water them –
And in some nondescript, un-opinionated, white-chrome
Future, we'll look back, but won't remember, only see
Behind us the same thing we see ahead: a vague mist,
Unfathomable fog of forgetting, our own Common Pact
Of Oblivion, our Very British *Olvido*, and austerity
Will be a distant myth (as all the premature deaths and
Suicides that footnoted it), a faint ancestral rumour,
Festering memory-tumour, a Ruritanian fantasy,
Something only dreamt as happening once upon another place
And time in a dystopian Uchronia of uninterrupted sleep…

14

As for austerity-spattered Spain, She will be given Her
Second *El pacto de Olvido* in the space of thirty-nine years,
And so soon after Socialist Prime Minister Zapatero
Officially relinquished the long-remembered first
With his Historical Memory Law, which made it no
Taboo anymore for the nation to remember
The countless casualties on both sides of the Civil War,
And those accrued during Franco's thirty-six year
Censorship, and for recriminations and post mortems
So long postponed to be taken up if any parties
Suspected historical crimes against humanity, atrocities,
Holocausts in those Locust Thirties, with particular
Emphasis on a formal denouncement of the Franco
Regime – Will they now be made to forget all this as well?
Be made to remember to forget all over again? Forget
Perhaps but never forgive: vast swathes of Spaniards
Today are calling for a new Republic, for getting rid
Of the Bourbons altogether, now that King Juan Carlos
Has abdicated, once seen as the saviour of Spanish
Democracy for granting free suffrage to the people
Again, on the death of diminutive, liquorish-moustached
Dictator, Franco – but whose conspicuous consumption
In the midst of his subjects' abject bankruptcy sickened
The famished Spanish – so many of whom reject his
Spit of a son, the Prince of Asturias' succession…

15

The Spanish never forget – in spite of patching Pacts,
Their past weighs heavy like red wine in the head,
Gleams in eyes like melted chocolate, remains ever-present,
Immanent, and sometimes they can smell it, taste it, touch it,
Hear it – a dry-throated hoarseness in flamenco singers'
Arabic cries, Rioja-coated rhotic of longing, the thump
Of gypsy-thrummed guitars, and in the slow drip-drip
Of bleeding green olives – and olives bleed green, ripe
Green juices let from veins of poverty's verboten young
Who've made their own private pacts of forgetting,
Opting for oblivion in the wake of democracy's
Rusty gauntlet slung down on the bull-ring dust
Like Don Quixote's glove, or Rupert John Cornford's
One slim posthumous volume – for now is not a time
For dreamers, romantics and idealists, but a time
For pragmatists and Sancho Panzas who mistakenly
See windmills instead of tilting Troika giants, who are
Deaf to the drip-drip of bleeding olives; for though
Those old rag-tag brigades are long disbanded in time,
And the Republic still trapped in retrospective aspic,
The isinglass of nostalgia's olive-brine, new red and green
Allegiances are seeding, and soon new olive branches
Will be thrusting from the Unión General de Trabajadores,
Los Indignados and Podemos (We Can), the Left victors
In Europe – together they give Spain one more hope of severing
The yoke that ties them to the Troika, for a reign of healing
Those olives old Donnelly once noticed were bleeding…

Red Generals

Rupert John Cornford, christened after Rupert Brooke, his
Unrelated 'uncle', posthumous patron, close friend of his poet-
Parents, Francis Macdonald and Frances Crofts Cornford,
Each initialled *'FMC'* and *'FCC'* to differentiate
Roles of engagement; but their brooding dusky son preferred
To be called by his middle name – perhaps to ward off a nominal

Jinx: angelic Rupert 'Chaucer' (Chawner) Brooke had passed onto
Olympus from Skyros, after sepsis from a mosquito bite –
Hence the titular transference, as if by tribute… Cambridge in
Nuptial season brought John seeding of ideas, desires, love and

Communist stirrings, a fierce romance with Margot Heinemann,
Oracle and Muse; then fathering 'James' with a Welsh girl called
Rachel Peters… But Spain stole his heart – or he volunteered it,
Not noticing, or caring, for the pattern of bullet-pattered *'R-u-p-e-r-t'*:
Fell among the Thaelmann battalion at Boadilla aged just twenty-
One-and-a-day – Esmond Romilly's homily… He'd no time for
'Red generals' of the POUM flashing sabres in recruiting bull-rings:
Dashing blazes to shaking leafs at the Front, songs and slogans wilting…

The Abandoned Shade

Laurie led a life before he wrote about it; took to the road – no
Aertex shirts, Pelican paperbacks, bicycles, greatcoats, torn
Umbrellas, prams piled up with bed sheets, or romps with
Rosy-cheeked girls in haystacks on a bellyful of scrumpy
Emptied from the barrel for this lad of Stroud and Slad,
Nothing but the road, the sprawling road for the son of an old
Celestial who never returned to his family after the War – only
England, Gloucestershire and absence; rejecter 'Reg' and the 'Lees',

Exiled from their hearts and thoughts – the distaff 'Lights', loved like cider;
Days dreamt away in red reveries at Veale Bracher's Tolstoyan
Whiteway Colony in the Cotswolds; then Sophia, a girl from
Argentina, inspired him to pack his trunk for Spain after she'd
Reticulated his tongue with a handful of Spanish words – he
Downed anchor first at Vigo, Pontevedra, and walked from

Almuñecar to Andalusia, surviving on his violin;
La Falange began its long grab for power precisely one summer
After Laurie's Spanish arrival… By '37, around when Andrés
Nin, founder of the POUM, was *'disappeared'* for Trotskyism,

Laurie volunteered with the International Brigades, but an
Absence seizure – *petit mal* – put paid to that… The GPO Film
Unit hired him as a scriptwriter during the Second World War;
Rose for winter – his bride, Catherine Francesca Polge (a Garman
Ingénue); hired as chief caption writer for the Festival of Britain;
Empty prizes and honours rolled like dominos on backs of books:

Land at War, The Sun My Monument, The Bloom of Candles – rubies
Ebbed from his perambulations; from the abandoned shade of green
England to blazing Spain – then the golden mean of a lamp-lit desk…

Greeks Bearing Rifts

*'And many a man whom fraud or law had sold
Far from his god-built land, an outcast slave,
I brought again to Athens; yea, and some,
Exiles from home through debt's oppressive load,
Speaking no more the dear Athenian tongue,
But wandering far and wide, I brought again;
And those that here in vilest slavery (douleia)
Crouched 'neath a master's (despōtes) frown, I set them free.'*
Solon, *Constitution of Athens* 12:4

1

Adulterated down the ages since Kleisthenes first sculpted it
Out of Athens' Doric bones, columns like trophy mammoth tusks –
But the dream was never completed, only mistranslated,
Doctored through the centuries by Draco's lasting tyranny
In drachmas (in spite of clashes of successive archons since):
Capital – parasitical carbuncle on democracy's milky body;
We carve out what we can from a millennium's penumbras
Cast in laundered light of invisible vested satellites,
Gilt-armoured Lacedaemonians who long ago avenged
The Sacred Band of Lovers – Thebes' brother-loving pederasts
Whose passions slew them – through arithmetical trickeries
To clinking aristocracies of antinomian lineages
Which adumbrate our histories pinched and plasticised by them –
So, today, Athena, whittled to Her tattered toga, crumpled
Under Europa, democracy's ancestral seat teetering
On bankruptcy – its Parthenon mortgaged to rum bar-
Barbarian ember days as bondage-states to shoulder-standing
Number-crunching giants, modern progenies of Vandals,
Visigoths and Teutons with Bismark-Kaiser fiscal spikes,
Kleptocratic pickelhaubes, Charlemagnic packages
Ringleted in chain-mails interlinked with Draconic clauses –
O how many gnarled Greek goat-herders tremble in their blood
With ancient legislations, their wine-skin faces soaked with age,
Brows of brown-earthed olive groves gripped in ruminations

On Classical ancestries, as if the pebbles Demosthenes
Gargled with to improve his speech-impediment for public
Oratory, was so much swilling in the wind: it all now seems
As botched, capricious and corrupt as the opportunistic course
Of Alkibiades' venal misadventures – traitor of Athens,
Defector to Sparta, then to Persia, then back again to Athens,
Tall tale twisting between his peripatetic legs – and what happened
To Alkibiades in the end? He shot out of his burning house
(Arson), a flame-tipped arrowhead hurtling untargeted
From its scorching quiver, distancing into satirical darkness –
An ancient Flashman smoked out by his own hubris,
His singed ancestral seat hissing to ashes in a water barrel;
From meteoric rise to whimsical caricature: and the same can
Be said of Democracy's much-trumpeted hyperbolic grotesque…

2

No doubt those hircine Hoplites, whose black olive eyes
Have seen this many melting times before – democracies
Foredoomed to shadow-coups – still wish, still hope for
Solon's ghost to come and still his bow-hand on fair justice,
For Hellas needs him now to shake all to its true foundations
Through shaking off of burdens, *Seisaktheia*, a reversal
Of fortunes, bouleversement, tax-Saturnalia, a turning
Upside down of lop-sided Order, not the shaking off of
The burdened as if They were the burdens; but cry stinking
Fish and *Seisaktheia*!; clean the nation's slate of debts, and
Root democracy deep as olive trees, or sculpt it pure,
Incorruptibly, from stone, stamp it in bas relief of marble
Rubric, inscribe it in blood, molasses-thick homologous
Haemoglobins, graft it into porous bone with labourers'
Matted sweat, weave it into tapestries of hair, purses sewn
From sinews, currencies from nerves, covenants codified
In toothcombs, the muscle and bone of a Greco Habeas
Corpus, self-ratifying skeletons sown by raging Argonauts
With dragons-teeth for automatic stabilisers – anything
To transplanted plutocracy, today's dole-slaves – *douleia* –
To bonds of barbed yield fields, or armies of underemployed
On zero-hours contracts; democracy market-floated,
Assets snapped up and stripped, captured in snatching fangs
Of capitalist Sultans farming pharmaceutical acres for
Further profits, Colchis bones of antidepressants thrown
To *hoi polloi* as pills of diminishing returns to soften moral
Blows; shelled out for song-bombed demos to forge new
Infrastructures of *'fiscal sustainability'*, auction psychic
Sovereignty – Greece, a fiscal Vassal State of Merkel's
Germany, Deutschland-on-the-Med, a nation of debt-
Slaves on the never-never credit slate and suffrage float…

3

All that's left for these fleeced children of Kleisthenes,
These inheritors of the most ancient democracy,
Is etched in marble tablets of Troika kleptocracy,
New Sparta's Austerity-Reuptake Inhibitors –
Though supplies are pitiful, depleting too rapidly for
Suicidal ideations; now Athens is the puppet-seat
Of plutocratic markets, a client state repaying ancient
Privileges in perpetual instalments at Wonga-like rates,
Olympus-high percentages, and taking out a mortgage on
The McAcropolis – a timocracy where few if any native
Greeks retain leases on pawned properties; a millennium
Behind its ancient advancements in culture and politics,
When Solon, the cultivated statesman, poet, law-giver
And aphorismic archon, announced his Constitution
Of Athens in iambic pentameter (a marriage of poetry
And politics not seen again in millennia, until English
Amateur poet, and prime minister, Clement Attlee) – today,
The Troika dictates its' colophon of Draconic demands
In brutal thumping prose which, if not complied with,
Will spill into more pugilistic Spartan call to arms against
Immigrants: legions of the Golden Dawn, Capitalism's
Last ditch shock-troops waiting in the thorny wings…

4

Now capitalism's tectonic plates crunch and scrape against
Each other, pit sister against brother in the struggle for
Survival, monetarist hegemonies and conglomerates
Sacking Greece, ancestral seat of democracy, all the way back
To Kleisthenes, now the most brutally betrayed by corporate-
Plumed, asset-stripping Peisistratids of cupidity
Clattering in on chariots: Athens atrophies, the Acropolis
Rocks to carpetbaggers, the Parthenon is pawned off
Like a mouldy heirloom, administrators and technocratic
Ostrogoths, protests and teargas, cuts and suicides,
New Spartans on the rise, *hoi barbaroi* no longer at the gates
But well inside, pumping in the blood of the race, poisoning
The wells while purifying the gene pool – beware Greeks
Bearing rifts: suntanned Fascists' branch-thrusting salutes –
Not the branches of olive trees but of oaks, those strong-
Armed brutes – arousing rigid hands, Swastika armbands,
Wolfsangels, gold eagle standards andpluming torches,
The Golden Dawn has no shortage of foreign scapegoats,
Or shaven-headed recruits, thuggish Siegfrieds and flaming
Parsifals… And yet it seems so out-of-kilter with a warmer
Climate for Fascism to spring up all of a sudden under
Such a bright and ancient sun – Whither the plumed phoenix
Of democracy? Whither the graceful swan? Whither the olive
Branch of *Seisakhtheia* held out by Solon? The shaking off
Of burdens through mass debt-wipe and dampening down
Of mythic deficits with new warmth of infrastructures,
The salvage of slaves into aspirational Strata of Thetes?
Nothing but Draconic Code of the Troika's fiscal
Consolidation, balancing of the crooks by kleptocrats;
Athenian Nazis talking shop, of making lampshades from skins
Of immigrants – Nationalism's new budget range of recyclable
Barbarians, burning libraries after borrowing wrong books…

5

Sanguine Lagarde, phlegmatic permatanned Madame de
Austérité, hostess of the IMF, beguiling while reclining
On her Louis XVI chaise-lounge, hardly a drag queen
Apropos Napoleon Bonaparte, she warned not long ago
Of *'another 1930s moment'*, as the drachma-scraping
Monetarist sipped from her champagne flute and berated
The Troika-shackled insolvent Greeks for complaining
About their abject poverty, adults going without regular
Meals in order to feed their children and pay for
Medical prescriptions for them, as the long shadow
Of Hippocrates crept perilously further away out
Of the harsh sunlight of the stomach-panging Agora,
They would have to sink to the lower depths of *'sub-
Saharan poverty'* before she would sympathise with them –
This lounging Olympian who can only grasp poverty
As an abstract, being the absolute opposite condition
To that afforded through her own gratuities, anything
In the grey in-between, impossible for her to fathom
Or empathise with (that would require emotional
Nuances not commonly known to punctuate caviar
And canapés of number-crunchers), since there always
Remains ambiguity as to its roots and causes – could
Be down to profligacy, *'fecklessness'*, *'idleness'*, *'poor life
Choices'*, moral loucheness; even Lutheran Angela Merkel
Flinched from parroting such hope-crippling rhetoric…

6

Now the Greeks are so many dice thrown across the roulette
Wheel of European plutocrats; Alexis Tsipras' Syriza
(Synaspismós Rizospastikís Aristerás almost; Coalition
Of the Radical Left) – a veritable Jason and the Argonauts
Against the might of the Troika, voyaging through the ever-
Impinging *symplegades* of the markets and their golden
Fleecing of the throttled Nation State – almost seized the day,
But not quite (*yet!*), though won a moral victory,
Made a stand against the fiscal blackmail of the markets'
Kleptocracy – and, since, has catapulted his party
Into the public consciousness of Greece (and two years
Hence, will lead them to their *Oxi* vote against further
Troika blackmail – true democracy in action? Sadly, no:
Democratic impotence, merely tokenistic elections, since
National capitulation to further austerity is once more
The 'only option on the table', 'no alternative' to buckling
To a coup of 'the forces of darkness' against democracy
As phrased by Caroline Lucas of the English Greens;
All this, the intellectually gifted Marxist finance minister,
Yanis Varoufakis, foresaw, hence his resignation in spite
Of the *Oxi* vote); while the Indignants at Syntagma are
Camped down for the long run and will not be intimidated
By stigma, nor be scattered by stings of rubber bullets or
Blasts of water canon… What matter the common people,
The plebs, *hoi polloi*, opposed to Troika timocracy
Imposed on their purely nominal democracy –
Supposed to be rule by the people, *hoi demos* – including
The unprecedented step to close down Greek state television
And its ERT radio station, *sans* any public consultation,
Even though both institutions are 'publicly owned' –
But in the scorching June of 2013 AD, Antonis Samaras,
Puppet prime minister handpicked by the markets,
Pinstriped ambassador for the Troika, makes his swift
Autocratic move, an anti-state broadcasting coup,
Silencing the ERT (on the airwaves unremittingly
Since the Thirties), state-funded through electricity bills –
Although not as reliably now that lights go out in Athens…

7

Greece is ever the seminal pilot of new types of state:
Ancestral seat of the first democracy, and, today,
Europe's first kleptocracy and credit-slate client-state –
Most of our English nouns are from the Ancient Greeks:
'Metropolitan', 'politics', 'plutocracy', 'philanthropy'... And
O O O Boris of the Britons urges euergetism,
Go get 'em evergetism – *good deeds* – among his young
Blond Turks in the City, asserting that mythical Smithian
'Invisible hand' of capitalism – a blank cheque signed
In invisible ink not worth the paper it's forged on –
But it's another round of shadow-boxing for Alexander
Boris de Pfeffel Johnson, great grandson of Ali Kemal Bey,
Once Interior Minister for Damat Ferid Pasha, Grand
Vizier of the Ottoman Empire – in the golden mean time,
While setting himself up as some kind of People's Emperor,
A Nero of Noblesse Oblige fiddling with his broom
While London burns, his buying up of water-canons from
The Turks' old allies, the Germans, presages a perfect storm
Of duplicity... And so, it seems, in spite of countless
Sacrifices at the altar of austerity, in all social senses
England will go the way of flagellated Greece, how it was
In that first swathe of swingeing blades which sparked off
Riots, firebombs and Molotov Cocktails rocking
The Acropolis outside the Klepto-Greek Parliament,
Where the Presidential Guard, the *Tsoliades, Evzones*
Of the Eurozone, prancing *Klephts* ('*Thieves*' of the Ottoman
Mountains) – and *Armatoloi*, Greece's so-called '*yeast
Of liberty*' – in their blowsy white *fustanella* kilts, scarlet
Fezzes with black tassels, garters, white woollen stockings
(*Periskelides*), and red leather clogs with black pompoms,
Perform their slow-motion march, occulting changing
Of the guard, military ballet, regimental mystique,
One leg rising effortlessly to eye-height then stomping down,
Repeat, repeat, unflinchingly... And they say a sign of madness
Is to keep doing the same thing again and again in hope
Of a different result, eventually (or perhaps Capitalists,
Like Carpocratians, simply seek to reach some unspecified
State of mortal perfection through accumulative material sin –

A fiscal Calvinism?), every parade drill is a ritual in
Scrupulosity painstakingly disciplined to kill all spontaneity;
And such repeat-behaviour is the default-mechanism
Of capitalism-in-crisis – from the Greek *krisis*: a critical
Moment of decision; if Trotskyism is the doctrine
Of permanent revolution, then Capitalism is the practice
Of permanent crisis, can operate no other way but in
Economic chaos, relies on chronic oscillations in
Supply and demand, slump and boom, needs unemployment
So it has a permanent rump of surplus would-be employees
By which to bargain wages down – calls this *'competition'*;
Manages antagonisms of a top quintile's conspicuous
Consumption amid mass penury – Capitalism is a clay
Ray Harryhausen Cyclops, a scaly grotesque whose single eye
Swivels envy-green for everything it wants but nothing
That it needs, mesmerised by its own ingrained commodity-
Fetishism, trapped in jolty footage on stop-motion repeat…
Repeat… repeat of its faulty profit default mechanism…
It is such animal energies long unleashed on the Greeks…

O Solon's country needs him now, by bow-hand and by plough…

The Green Heart of Germany
(Thuringia Tiger)

*on the triumph of the 'Red-Red-Green' Centre-Left
in the Landtag of Thuringia election 2014*

Thuringia, thick-forested, the green heart of Germany,
Has never been so green as it is today – for the *'Daily
Miracle'* (the *Morning Star*) proclaims *'Red-Red-Green is
Triumphant in Thuringia'* and by just one single *'wavering vote'*,
Which catapulted the Left Party, Die Linke, to sit atop
Its progressive counterparts – the Social Democrats and
Greens – in the Landtag of Thuringia, as the crest of this
Socialist Coat of Arms, *gules, seven mullets of six points argent*,
Superimposed over the arms of the Landgraves (*azure,
A crowned lion rampant barry of eight argent and gules, crown
And claws or*, since the 13th century) in 1920 –
Promptly de-mantled under the Nazis in 1933;
But now those arms are *gules, seven mullets of six points vert* –
For it's Red-Red-Green in Thuringia, Left in the Federal
Free State, West-shunting in Weimar, leaning East again
In the land of Bach, Goethe and Schiller; it's Red in
The green heart of Germany, Red as it's ever been,
Thuringia in glorious Green and Red, a forest refuge
From conflagrations of a Continent's right-wing intransigence
And rising dogma of permanent austerity, its' lacerating
Fiscal claws – a pause for thought for Angela Merkel
And the Troika: none had reckoned for this counter-hegemonic
Clause in default democracy that voters would endorse
A confederacy of oppositionists for its' state administration,
And time can only tell if this will be a mouse that roars,
But much thunder has been known to rumble from such common cause;
And this red-striped green Thuringia Tiger promises
Munificent menace, prowling in the midst of capitalism,
Paws sharpening the more austerity's cheetah mauls,
For it's an insurgent wild cat of sorts, *barry of eight vert and gules* –

Germany might lead the swingeing hegemonies of Europe's
Monetarist marauders beating the Continent blue
Until it's back in the black, but the reigning nation has
A thoroughly green heart and it's heating up like forest tinder…

**Red
Wilderness**

When is a Red Swede a Beetroot?

Job to job and by and by – third of nine children born to
Olof Hägglund, conductor on the Gefle-Dala railway line
Sprawling Sweden West-to-East, and Margarita Catharina; Joel
Emmanuel, by birth name, one of six to see adulthood;
Paul, one of his brothers, accompanied him to America,
Hired cheap as labourers; there Joel changed his name to Joseph

Hillström after signing up for membership with the
Industrial Workers of the World – the *'Wobblies'*, so
Labelled – in his birth name, to avoid anti-union black-
Listing; later, he shortened it to 'Joe Hill' when signing his
Socialist poems, protest songs, speeches, lampoon-hymns,
'The Preacher and the Slave' – *'pie in the sky'* was his phrase:
Riff on the Salvation Army number 'In the Sweet By-and-By',
O mercy, 'Casey Jones – Union Scab', and other popular
Melodies… Hill's ill-starred banner was his twilight's last gleaming:

A ricochet incriminated him: ex-policemen, John G. Morrison,
Killed in a shooting, along with his son, by men in red bandanas…
Afterwards, Hill hobbled up to his doctor's doorstep wobbling

Jelly-limbed, red of a bullet wound blotting his shirt like beetroot
Over his left lung: he claimed he'd been shot, over a Hilda
Eriksson, by a jealous rival, Otto Appelquist, but it was too close to

Home for comfort or coincidence: both incidents linked: Hill,
Indicted and found guilty – no bids for clemency from
Luminaries Woodrow Wilson, Helen Keller, the Swedish Embassy,
Let him off the firing squad the following November… When

'Ready, aim – ' was called, he volleyed back *'Fire – go on fire!'*
In a socialist paper, *Appeal to Reason*, he'd opined he was the
Perfect scapegoat: a tramp, a Swede, but worst of all, a *'Wobbly'*…

Where's Wal?

Where's Wal? Walter Hannington? 'Wal' to his close comrades
And well-rewarded readerships; old Red Dog of Gollancz'
Left Book Club's pimply orange rinds – he pumped out heaps of books,
Two pumpkins of polemic every other year, squashed in end-to-
End by khaki bookends; between airships and doodlebugs his words
Roared through the Cocktail Twenties, and blew their shrieking

Whistles on social holocausts throughout the Thirsty Thirties:
A conscientious protector of his pauperised priceless species;
Lemuel Gulliver of Lilliput Proles, champion of the unemployed

(Helots of the Western World) and howling-bellied working poor:
An Exposure of the Unemployed Social Schemes; Work for Wages,
Not Slave Schemes; Ten Lean Years; How to Get Unemployment Benefit;
Never On Our Knees; Black Coffins and the Unemployed – Wal took
In the washing of the great unwashed, rinsed it through the wringer;
Navigated the *Distressed Areas* – polemical Marco Polo…
Gongs never sounded, no CBEs for the CPGB's co-founder,
Totem-mouth of the National Unemployed Workers' Movement;
Old Bailey jailbait: sent down for *'Incitement to Mutiny'* –
No porridge put him off: struggle's gruel agreed with his belly…

Thaxted Redux

1

Once upon a time in a Uchronia of unicorns and socialists,
There was a magical Parish in Uttersford, Essex,
And, though shrouded in shire mists of crimson rumours
And Sino whispers, the mythical town of Thaxted
Actually existed, even if today it's only there in name
And vestige – but in its Uchronian heyday, Thaxted
Was a political outpost of the sea-green heritage
Of English radicalism, underground ideas of Lollards,
Diggers, Levellers, Jacobins, Luddites, Chartists,
And permanent revolutions of organ voluntaries:
The parish was taken under the jackdaw-wing
Of a radical cleric with an audaciously Continental
Name hung with Huguenot mystique: Conrad le
Despenser Roden Noël, the so-called *'Red Vicar'* or
'Turbulent priest… of Thaxted', a thorn in the sides
Of both Tory and Liberal prime ministers from Balfour
To Chamberlain – Thomas Á Becket to Stanley Baldwin's
Fulminating Curtmantle; all rendered more mediaeval
To the shuddering grinds of Noël's surrogate organist,
Gustavus Theodore von Holst (also of thoroughly
Foreign-sounding name and Scandinavian-Baltic ancestry,
A quarter Swedish, via Riga, Latvia), his favourite
Composer-cum-parishioner, and fellow socialist…

2

By this time, Noël busied himself in non-liturgical duties,
As a founding member of the British Socialist Party
And core Anglican founder of the Catholic Crusade
That first pitched Trotskyite thought in the foggy change-
Resistant shires of England – a polemical rhetorician,
As illustrated in a transcript from his public dialogical
Joust with Frank Jannaway, a Christadelphian, who
Put forth a reactionary thesis, *A Godless Socialism*,
To which Noël's oppositional riposte was, *'Ought Christians
To be Socialists?'*; billed as a *'Debate with the 'Red Vicar'
Rev. Conrad Noël'*, in 1909… The Crimson Curate
Incurred the rugger-aggro of Cambridge undergraduates
After he'd hung the Red Flag and Sinn Féin's beside
St. George's in Thaxted Church – Noël lost the ensuing
'Battle of the Flags': was forced to take both banners
Down by edict of the consistory court – this incident,
By way of anti-climax, together with Noël's torrid
Priesthood to date, inspired spark-eyed craggy actor
Robert Shaw's prize-winning novel, *The Flag*… But
The only posthumous trophies Noël coveted were beacons
Of red flags in place of St. George crosses on every
Hilltop in England, embedding red tidings in flint
Hearts and mossy minds of green-eyed Englishmen…

3

By the restive, recession-hit Thirties, Noël was not entirely
Alone in his clerical red-leanings: Cosmo Gordon Lang,
Antifascist Archbishop of Canterbury, publicly denounced
The flattening of Guernica by German bombs, at a time
When Stanley Baldwin's National Government was
Vacillating between strategic interests and a tacit attraction
To nascent Hitlerism – although Cosmo fell short of arguing
For British intervention on the side of the Spanish Republic,
Along with the lion's share of Parliament – and later,
By dint of his pacifism, supported Neville Chamberlain's
Paper-fluttering attempt at Appeasement… There was
More than a mere trend at this time for a merging
Of Christian and Communist thought hinging on the coign
Of vantage in Anglicanism: Cosmo's own second-in-charge,
Hewlett Johnson, acquired the legend of *'The Red Dean
Of Canterbury'* for his championing of the Soviet Union
And his authoring of *The Socialist Sixth of the World* –
A Left Book Club tome published by Victor Gollancz
In 1939… But Cosmo was no liberation theologian, nor,
Specifically, a socialist, no long-distance idealist as was
Thaxted's rusticating recalcitrant cleric; instead, he reclined
With age into a balding small-c Conservative, a Stanley
Baldwin cast-off with crook-staff and cassock, whose
Impromptu alopecia had intercepted his formerly youthful
Countenance for all the pricks of his capricious Archbishopric,
Which culminated in his dummy of dotage being ritually
Burnt like a Guido Fawkes effigy by conflagrations
Of farmers for his defence of the ancient status quo
Of churchly taxes on agricultural incomes during
The *'Tithe Wars'* – O, such a comedown from greener
Ideological days when he'd cut a dash in Radical Cloth,
And, as a Lord Spiritual, voted against the Peers' attempts
To pettifog Lloyd George's *'People's Budget'*: Cosmo's maiden
Speech berated the Second Chamber's ermined *'unwisdom'*
In vetoing those progressive measures – thus making his
Mark, in spite of being rebuffed by Tory, Lord Curzon…

4

In any case, history was on Cosmo's side in this heated
Debate – even if his aging conscience wasn't: Herbert
Asquith's Government called the bluff of the Temporal
Billy Goats Gruff with a snap General Election in January
1910, securing a mandate for raising taxes on the rich
In order to fund new welfare for the poorest – a veritable
'Robin Hood Budget'… In spite of his quiescent autumn,
Cosmo set a precedent in his surplice spring, since taken
Up by outspoken Archbishops of Canterbury,
A rhetorical robustness against unchristian injustices,
Recapitulated by Robert Runcie's attitudinal opposition
To Thatcherism in the Demiurge Eighties, and, latterly
Ricocheting in the twenty-first century, against the restraints
Of muscular hegemonic smokescreens, Archbishops
Of Canterbury Williams and Welby, and Archbishop
Of York, Sentamu, have kept up the radical tradition
Of polemical clericalism, Christian Socialism,
Lifted the mitre of altruism, hoisted the crosier of social
Conscience, spoken up for the poor precisely at a time
When politics-spun preconceptions are at their all-time
Iciest towards *'the undeserving'*, and contrapuntal
'Public opinion' (red-top parroting) is flint-hearted
Towards welfare claimants, human sympathy worn thin
Towards the disadvantaged – at best, coldly phrenological,
At worst, chillingly eugenicist, tartly Malthusian…

5

But at least the Church of England is emphatically
No more *'the Tory Party at prayer'*, has begun to shake
Off the cobwebbed nebulousness of noblesse oblige
And establishmentarianism, cast off the fetters of more
Suspect traditions, and, as if scraping its' hoary throat
Clear of accumulated dust that long coated its' vocal cords,
Rediscovered its' Roundhead disdain for privilege,
Its' tan serge tunics and metaphorical cropped hair,
Recognising again its' long-forgotten fondness for
Underdogs, and the seeds of dissent from which it sprouted –
Cathars, Lollards, Huguenots, Waldenses, Puritans, Ranters,
Shakers, Quakers, Millenarians – embedded deep within
Its long-neglected legacy of English recalcitrance,
An angry religion grown from barebones, ribs, rump and
Compost of Reformations, out into profuse offshoots –
Baptist, Anabaptist, Methodist, Presbyterian, and
Analgesic Anglican – so long the Church of the Establishment,
Bowdlerised by parsonages and regal patronage –
But now returning to its roots and original vision,
Putting the spirit of protest back into *Protest*antism…

Cuttslowe Walls

Clive Saxton was a castle-builder: in 1934,
His Urban Housing Company built turreted brick walls
Two metres high, topped with metal spikes so residents
Of his private homes were spared the eye-sore
Of the City Council's *'slum-dwellers'* next door;
Abe Lazarus, a Communist, took up the council tenants' cause,
'Bill Firestone', his comrades' sobriquet for him, for having
Waged and won a strike against the Firestone Rubber Company…

But the Cuttslowe Walls were too thick for his pickaxe of principle:
Abe was barred by the coppers before he could wield his blow –
Lo, in '38, the Council knocked it down, and so
Litigation came, and Saxton's wall went up again;
But a score on, in '59, compulsory purchase took a pickaxe to it…

Let this tale be a lesson to us at this time of wrecking-balls,
Of *'gentrification', 'doughnut ghettoes', 'dog-end voters'*
Rhetorically ignored (as opposed to *'respectable, lace-curtain poor'*),
A society which builds metaphorical partitions
Will only lose itself in a labyrinth of trapped moral miasma
With no way out but with a wrecking-ball – for every wall
There is a wrecking-ball, but the more cuts and caps chip away
At the narrowest shoulders under the weight of number-
Crunchers in Whitehall, the higher will stack our Cuttslowe Walls,
Until their Babel bricks prove unsupportable
And tumble, burying the builders under their own rubble…

Wootton Bassett

A centipede of disruptive pattern camouflage fatigues
Crawls through Wootton Bassett's buff-and-bereted streets,
Pallbearers in desert rigs, each pair of shoulders knees
Of a gigantic booted centipede trooping from the Giant Peach,
Each trunk one of a thousand two-pronged legs along
Which Union Jack-draped coffins undulate like rolling logs,
Or tropical leafs magnified on backs of soldier ants –
The bunting strung out in corresponding colours:
Red for spilt blood, white for corpses, blue for bruises,
Invisible bruises – riots of contrast in this consumerist realm
Of lotteries, forgotten histories, *With Sympathies*, foreign
Cruises through warmer waters increasingly contracting
From the fractious Middle-East to the scorched coast of Somalia;
Barely the room for these genteel ceremonies amid so many
Scarab Springs – and now, in this Afghanistan Autumn,
A pall finally falls upon the picturesque face of an ancient
Street in a sleepy Wiltshire parish replete with wilting wreaths,
Flags on caskets, rags on horns, corn dollies, scorned doleys;
But a prestigious gash of bloodied ennoblement is left
Behind in that dormant dormitory town, a congealed wound
Encrusting into bluemantled epithet: *'Royal'* Wootton Bassett…
'At the going down of the sun and in the morning we will remember'
When our Empire was a permanent sunset, a pounding
Interloper that, unlike Rome, didn't fall but dismantled
Itself into a Commonwealth under pragmatic slit-eyed
Clement Attlee, pencil-moustached emancipator
Of turbaned multitudes, prime colophon for pith-helmeted
Blimps of imperial India… At Remembrance and on
Armed Forces Day we will bite our tongues out of respect,
As our tears silently sting us; together we will salute
A khaki sunset which will rise next day in spite of us,
As traumatised veterans retch into sinks in unsung mornings;
While in our nation of novices that venerates *'hard work'*
As the cardinal virtue, we will be strangely discouraged
From celebrating International Workers' Day each 1st May,

The non-observance of proletarian spring will be corroborated
By an absence of bunting, for the red flag's branded a banner
Of unpatriotic surrender to foreign influences – fellowship,
Commonality, solidarity, equality, etcetera – and elicits
Nostril-seething enmity from hoof-stamping John Bull, by Jingo –
All break ranks and scatter as he bolts through Wootton Bassett
Brandishing an air-rifle, in a rage, on the rampage
Of a very different page, Reds and Rags to the slaughter;
Meanwhile, on market day the townspeople slip up on
The red crushed flesh of a machete-split watermelon…

Red Flag to a Bulldog

The rose-tinted-spectacled, bespoke Trotskyite
Come from somewhere '*up North*' to convert converted
Southerners ever further left, punctuated his
Apricot dialectics with '*And so on and so forth*',
And said with nostalgic glints gilding his optical rims:
'*My image of true working-class solidarity: the after-shift*
Pints shared by two labourers in brick-dusted donkey jackets
Propped up at a bar shoulder to shoulder, passing a fag
Between them with the bashful intimacy of covert lovers' –
Then smiled with triumph at his aphorismic flourish
As he sipped at a blonde ale in a throbbing pub's
Backstreet sabbatical for lubricated Bachelors
Imbibing bitter-tasting golden Belgian respite –
Textbook Bolsheviks with stool-cropped knees;
Turntable Trots spinning permanent revolutions
On waxing tongues, spiked principles like ice picks…

The pair of labourers he'd conjured, remained there,
In my imagination, elbow-propped at the bar,
Burley as nimbuses in grimy blue togs, cloth caps
Crimping their scalps like piecrusts; homing
Pigeons puffed up just to deflate with tarred lungs,
Fail to rise into radical action from coops
Of impotence, burst to shrunk balloons, let down
Like punctured tyres, sagging red flags subsumed
In John Bull burps and Union Jack bunting, collapsing
To barrages of sighs after barrels of exhausted laughter,
Militancy sinking into misty pints and cloudy eyes,
Browned-off buns by the dozen in an oven left open
To cool off the dough till the toughest crusts soften…

But they'll still be mumbling betimes by muggy beers –
In-between trumped mottos, *'Better Bread than Red'* –
That *'if'* and *'when'* the balloon goes up and the foghorn
Eeyores for *'The'* Revolution they've so woozily loved
Through inebriated sobs of obviation, wooed
Under many a down-tooled moon, they'd be among
'The first' punters to spring up from their pints and throw
In their weight with *'the young 'uns'*, string up *'the hoity-
Toity toffs'* and turnpike politicians (*'heads on spikes,
Heads or tails'*), throttle the mangy bulldog by its own
Choking chain, along with the pink-raw pit bulls
Of the snarling BNP; and while they're at it, put
A boot up the obsolete boneless backside of *'wobbly
Bloody Labour'*, put some Corbyn Red back in its jelly,
Less of the *'namby-pamby'* pink Milliband blancmange;
Before more of their purpling pals trip into the plum
Plush of aubergine-tinged Nigel Farage's no holds barred
Saloon bar, burbling on about *'Jam tomorrow, jam
Tomorrow'* – Ukip if you want to, but these old comrades
Aren't for kipping, nor for rolling up the blunt red banners
Of their tongues like pinstriped City men's umbrellas,
More for rolling up their sleeves for a good knuckling,
A bunch of fives with new *'blue-collar Conservatives'*,
Black eyes and bruises for five more bloomin' blue years…

Sloping home pie-eyed and empty-pocketed they'll be
Slurring *'Though cowards flinch and traitors sneer,/We'll keep
The red flag flying here'*, proudly thumping beetroot hearts,
Until their stupors rupture into burps, sighs and grunts
To be shrugged off in fag-singed armchairs grown from
Black roots of ropey slippers' carpet-planted plantains –
Wet green tongues rinsed of soggy red song through
Another sloshing night's mangle-wrung nostalgia…

Taser Dawn

Basildon tabard brigade's Away Day rallied at Dale Farm
With clamps and battering rams under banners of the Big
Quick Cement Society... No kiss of the blarney marks
Charmless masks of Billericay bailiffs and basilisks
Tattooed with tax discs, rakers of self-harming greenfields'
Congealing scars of mud camps; no coupon popery
Of tinkers from Tipperary or rubs of verbal rosaries
Over smoky tongues of patchwork Catholics can cockle-warm
Cemented hearts, nor dancing Mica stares of caravan-
Travellers catch light on helmets' melted candle-stumps...
Irish eyes are dialling ambulances, bruising black, clocking
Miles, arrested in transits like winkles in isinglass,
Sacramental brows sunless as shaving mirrors... Barnacled
Recusants reincarnated – through poorly parked karma –
Into Calvinist austerities and fractious clocks' back Black-and-
Tan anathemas, ancestral repeats recaptured on cameras:
Trans-Saxon expansions into wilting Celtic Twilights
On behalves of feral elites, Sheridan Clans cleared out from
Enclosures, refugees of petrol-grimed shores... Roll back
Bollard days: Robin Greenbreasts, Scarlet Hoods, Brown Jackdaws
And roofless House Martins branching out on iron boughs
Of makeshift Sherwood Forests grown from scaffolding,
Patrolled by episcopacies of *'Crusties'* shadowed by placard-
Carrying recruits to drastic chic: *'anti-capitalists'* – ripe
Fruit for craning cherry-pickers and grasping Hydraladders...

Police crash in at thwack of dawn: fuming magpies in damson
Morions, thunderstorms of Ironsides in riot visors
Triggering strings of static lightning, crackling Damascuses
Of Scarab Springs sparking papists to faradised genuflections,
Halted in halting site – O yellow-plastic parasites,
Holstered daffodils of yoyoing Triffid-stings! No fulgurites
Of emptied pellets left behind after tidy Taserings...

Camp flat-packed to scrap in damp autumn morning:
A rust-screeching wrecking-ball slings the mist like a thurible
Spraying incense – a Masonic Council's magic ritual:
Shrubs and bollards abracadabra back to rubble
And Chubbs of Conquest's portacabins... No tar-tongued
Catechisms or peeling Virgin Maries sprung
In upended bath-tubs like unearthed shrines – Armitage
Shanks' *'Almar Mater'* range – repels purges; no bunches
Of rusty heather arranged under bruised umbrellas
Of nettle-let wrists in porcelain slabs thrust up to ruptured
Surfaces, arrest greenbelt grabs; no hoisted crosses
Or torched cars curb pincer-movements on slummy uplands,
Nor banish black triangles slung on punched-up number plates...

Sobering ablutions bulge in fat buff envelopes
And Starbucks frappuccinos slurped on Browncoat couches
Of Hugo Boss NIMBY-beige... Final Score: *'Gyps'* and *'Micks'*:
Evicted/ Basildon Council: Text-communicate...

Ash Friday

The lights are out in Whitechapel but brick-lit beacons glow –
When torches burn for *'freedom'*, the books are first to go,
They catch at Fahrenheit Four Five One (as all fascists know),
Still time for speed-readers to trace the blackening tomes,
Appreciate combustible sentiments before the crows
Flap their crackling wings to ashes as the plumed flames grow
Into a white-hot dove, the burning bird, Whitechapel's ghost
Waxing in its blazing nest until bell, book and hose
Wash the conflagration – singed bookshelves, rows on rows
Splutter up their hissing dampblack pamphlets of scorched prose –
Peace-promoting posters on plaster walls, burnt and glozed
Like smudged thumbmarks on blank pages of churchly brows
At Ash-Wednesday; the ceiling, charred and traumatised, so
Its surface has a fractured ashy tarnish like a monochrome
Mosaic, a charcoaled Pompeii relic, almost black, like shadow,
Or liquorish – an ecliptic sunset burnish stains the oak
Wood wall supports – firebombed freedom billows up in smoke:
Like burning abbeys, or *'benefit cheat'* red-top tabloid tropes –
But who has lit the tinder? Those blue-touch tongues that throw
Torches of scorching rhetoric over the Westminster moat
From behind that forked portcullis? Fireproof MPs know
It only takes a waft of parliamentary papers to fan the flow
Of incendiary opinion until it singes the bloodhound nose
Of a reactionary fanatic, a backstreet blackshirt Guido
And his Orcish contrarians, out to burn a dodo,
Sniff out Crusties' refuges, pokey foxed pockets of hope,
Those little shops of peacenik-prop that stock a wider scope
Of typed perceptions outside Tory tittle-tattle *Metro*s,
And rotten chestnut *Evening Standard*s vendors hand to droves
Of pressed-for-time commuters who'll grab whatever goes,
Blue-top sops to mop myopic brows from Bank to Bow,
Coarsely varnished truths that glaze their brains to egg-brushed dough –
Fascism always starts small, acorns of resentment closed
To themselves, unconscious conches, polished till they glow
And swell into ectopic shrubs then mushroom into oaks,

Spread their sinuous branches out with hands that cannot close
But stamp the air in raised salutes as boots stamp on burnt toes –
Amber warnings abound now like luminous traffic cones,
How close must we all come before the glaring mirage shows
It is no mirage, but a timebomb rumour about to blow –
When torches burn for *'freedom'*, the books are first to go –
We must stamp out the flames before they catch so all those
To follow us in future look back through blown-out windows
To see that out of Ash Friday Whitechapel's phoenix rose…

Coventry Blue

Thatcher's Statue

The mystique-thicketed City of London Cult erected
A statue of Margaret Hilda Thatcher in sculpted marble
And set it in a Romanesque recess, a grotesque parody
Of a Roman goddess, one arm slung through a handbag-strap –
A posthumous addition to the monetarist pantheon,
One of the more controversial vestals of the Novensides;
And in the hoary tradition of classical iconoclasm,
The statue was decapitated by one 'Mr. Kelleher'
With the pressure of a metal rope support stanchion
And the swing of a Slazenger V600 cricket bat –
So off rolled the hard white head, its' adamantine mane of snakes
Still intact; the Ostrogoth, looking on the decapitated
Face of his act without fear of petrifaction, was, nonetheless,
Prosecuted and sent down promptly, in spite of his act being
The ultimate tribute to an autocrat; Kelleher struck
A symbolic blow, ritual deconstruction of a porous myth
Hardening into hand-bagged hagiography, marbling
'Maggieography', grabbing bogus glory, a snatch at lasting
Narrative: her graven image had to be traumatised, chipped
Away a bit – on that he was merely curtailing a rhetorical
Prophecy of Thatcher's future sanctification, cast in stone:
'Mrs Thatcher clearly regards herself as a deus ex machina,
Sent down from on high to 'knock Britain into shape'. She will
Wield her power…dictatorially and without compunction…
There is a tremendous danger…in believing that 'Thatcherism'
Is somehow now invincible, that it has established a new consensus
And that all the rest of us can do is debate alternatives within
Its framework. It is essential to demythologise 'Thatcherism'…
Thus Spake Blairasthustra back in 1987 – the rest, as his
Apparatchiks would say, was *'The Third Way'*…
As to whether her effigy should be inaugurated in Grantham,
The unassuming town on the River Witham in Lincolnshire,
Where she was grown, cultivated from cuttings of Samuel
Smiles' *Self-Help* and selective Victoriana potted by her

Shopkeeper father; while the beneficiaries of 'Right to Buy-
To-Let' Basildon are bidding for her marble beatification
In their bought-off borough... But Thatcher's statue already
Stands in every town and city, has for over thirty years,
In panoply of shapes: the scooped-out Co-op department
Store asset-stripped TO LET, the betting shop, the pawnbrokers,
The *CASH FOR GOLD* exchange, the gastro pub, jobcentreplus,
The temping agency, the A4e, the Atos sickness-cannery,
The soup kitchen, the food bank's alfresco buffets of tins
And cans in every backstreet, the *'homeless spikes'*, the *'poor doors'*,
The pitched *Big Issue* vendor, the hectoring cherry-tops,
The obsolete hope in the porchway wino's bloodshot eyes,
The scaffolding stacked up against each derelict human building
Of never-finished characters paying mute tributes to her
Scarring legacy; and so passionate are these supplicants,
They kneel on cardboard prayer rugs – pulled from under them –
On scum-caked pavements, glazed in grime, palms cupped
For alms, donations to her germy memory that swells through
Their obscurity and footnote-destitution, until their inks
Smudge away; they pay the daily price for her giant leap
To Finchley through one long sacrificial graze in the shadow
Of her sowreignty – many are statues themselves, indigent
Effigies, stone-struck cast-offs from her sculpting swage,
Petrified Mr Tumnuses, gnarled ornaments in Gorgons' sunken
Gardens, arranged like damaged goods under her marble glare...

Glossolalia

1
Tongue to tongue the new-strung language
Wound in ambages
Incomprehensible to some,
Untranslatable to teeth ground down
To candle-stumps
Congealed in red-wax seals of bleeding gums
Rose red blood undone
Between teeth and tongue
Slid coinages
Palm to palm
Crumb to crumb
As Tories and evangelists
Held euphoric Eucharists
Bodies into bread
Sharp teeth into Tongues
Totems of torches and tambourines
Insurmountable symbols
Bitter-tasting medicines
To apostates and unbelievers
Socialists and obsoletes
Neither ways held aught solutions
For all those in material need
In the age of 'respectable greed'

2

At those ecstatic rallies unfathomable banners hung
Forbiddingly as blue-midnight Berlin drapes beneath that giant
Flaming Torch, occulting totem of that Cartesian Creed
Of moral dualism, called *'Conservatism'* – What did it *mean*?
Con-ser-va-tive? To *conserve?* Conserve *what* precisely? –
And *Tory*, their nickname, that almost chimed with Torah,
But derived from the Irish *tóraidhe*, meaning outlaw, robber
Or brigand (but O no Strawberry Thieves!) from the Irish root *tóir*,
Which denoted *pursuit*, or *pursued men* – but it was us who were
Pursued by Them, hunted down by fence-posts of manifestos,
All those who didn't agree with that fractious rhetoric,
Uncompassionate polemic, acquisitive dialectic, the grasping
Pursuit of Profit, Mammon-tipped, the serpentine shibboleth
Of *'entrepreneurialism'*, the cryptic sanctification
Of *'animal spirits'* through *'competition'*, old Social Darwinism;
Semantic daggers poking through the closing cloaks of the young-
Up-and-coming cut from the cloth of an ancestral Right Club,
Oral sacraments in ranting choruses of Capitalist Magnificat,
And social intolerance cut in walnut Malthusianism,
Catapulted from contrapuntal tongues of youth's Teutonic
Apprentices, blond boys in razor-sharp suits who seemed
So furiously *free* – but if free, why so angry? *Free* to be
Shopkeepers, bank managers, pawnbrokers, loan sharks,
Anything they wanted or could imagine within the artificial
Limitations of material reality, cash-card authenticity –
That Carpocratian breed; the primal pursuit of property
And capital, penthouse suites, pyramid schemes, corporate piles,
As if to distract themselves from ill-expressed existential
Death anxieties, or the false belief that somehow money
Could purchase shares in immortality… From what some of us
Could see, this ascendant fiscal faith thrust self-interest, greed,
Avarice, acquisitiveness, one-upmanship, wolfish opportunity
To the fore, carried vestments of investments; no mercy for
Those who refused to succumb, trip up others in the race to
Worship at the altar of this intractable tract of attitude,
'Thatcherism', as it came to be named after its shop-proprietor,
Margaret Hilda Thatcher, Oxford-groomed daughter grown
By a grocer from Grantham who wove Victorian values

Into her thoughts' worsted fabric – her creed *'made greed
Respectable'* again; and those who still spoke in the obsolete
Tongue of *'One Nation'*, Community, Cooperation, Socialism –
All such dissenters and recusants still touched by symptoms
Of a more compassionate post-war consensus, were persecuted
In spirit by Thatcherism's snatching atmospherics –
It represented not a *'change of heart'*, but a faulty transplant…

3

There was something primal in that almost-hysteria
Of those highly charged rallies as those that had fifty or
So years before intoxicated Thirties German neuroticism
Rumbustiously choreographed fascist ranting of a gassed,
Traumatised Austrian Corporal who'd won the Iron Cross,
And coasted homeless from doss house to soap box;
And those flaming torches throbbing in nocturnal marches
Goose-stepping through evening streets in Berlin and Nuremberg;
Something of that harsh rationalism so disposed to irrational
Demagoguery at those intoxicated conferences
Of the teeth-edged Eighties – the stacking waves of cornflower
Blue, the muscularly flexing blue flag trumping the red,
Sailing obstreperously in the conditioned air by the hand
Of that ferocious lioness of rhetoric with lemon-meringue
Mane – that snarling, matriarchal figurehead, Aslan's
Intractable sister breathing icicles of acquisition across
A patchwork Narnia – fiercer than the Snow Witch,
The Iron Lady's tundra was scattered with petrified resistors
To her Gorgon's glare… At those torch-lit rallies, designed
To intimidate all opposition while hypnotising partakers,
After the spokespersons had extemporised their raptures,
All waved frantic Jacks, singing 'I Vow to Thee My Country',
Cecil Spring Rice's insipid lyric to the pastoral passage
From socialist composer Gustav Holst's 'Jupiter',
Which the quarter-Swedish maestro had christened 'Thaxted'
After the Essex village where he'd sojourned among
The fellowship surrounding Conrad Noel, the '*Red Vicar*' –
Holst must have been spinning in his orbit as those Tories
Milked his composition for empty patriotism (so many
Planetary-imposter Plutos); sometimes they'd even thump
Out William Blake's revolutionary anthem 'Jerusalem'
To the mawkish strains of Hubert Parry's hymnodic score,
Intoning '*And did His feet/ In ancient times/Walk upon
England's mountains green…*' in puerile interpretation,
But symbolic transplantation… Those Thatcherites spoke a collective
Glossolalia, New Tongues, which only they understood,
At least, initially, but which would prove infectious
To the Many, as a virus, a germ spreading contagiously

In the blue heat, a rapacious bacteria with grasping claws,
Corrupting communities with carrots of Right-To-Buy schemes,
While yuppies and guppies glorified gerunds, *'enterprising'*,
'Capitalising', buoyed on endorphins of opportunism,
Speculation, pyramid scams – filofaxes and portable phones,
Their ideological emblems… Oh, there were some who
Couldn't brook such bare-faced avarice and acceleration
Of get-rich-quick rat races at the expense of the less materially
Resilient – for those socialistically inclined recusants
None of it echoed any moral commonality, but blared
Like hunting bugles in the ears of numbers-blind urban foxes,
Roared its' gory fanfares of fiscal fallacy and grab-all
Amorality, all soft touches and bleeding hearts were in for
A decadal mauling; their deeply held convictions, proscribed
Opinions, chronically offended, those many who then were
Without a voice for all the clamour of venal ventriloquism…

4

While socialism was in decline after discontented winters
(Setting in with unshiftable snowdrifts of national mythology,
Of union bogeymen and closet-Trotskyite Kite-like closed-shop
Stewards with views as narrow as their pencil-thin moustaches –
Perceived as spivs of industry, red racketeers), the general
Choice of contrapuntal moralism, not opposition but
Distraction from the new rampant materialism, was in
Resurgent evangelicalism, the *'Born Again'* Christians,
Trooping on *'Make Way'* marches through knotted creels
Of Cornish fishing villages, rustling tambourines – or in cities,
Thumping Bibles in grubby faces of cardboard faithless,
Rejoicing *'He Lives'* in a society where *'He'*, above all others,
Would have been calling for a faithful Opposition to the blueing
Tide of regressive greed, and throwing out the money-lenders
From Paternoster's temples… But, seemingly, His followers,
His modern-day evangelists, contemporary apostles
And disciples thought it best to celebrate his Word in rustic
Chapels with priests in turtlenecks strumming acoustic guitars
To gregarious congregations of hand-clapping parishioners,
Holding up their palms to grasp at godly energies generated
In the body-heat of epileptic chapels, blood-bone-and-sinew
Believers, eyes shut, smiles of beatific almost sexual glee
Beaming across believing faces, raptures of waving palms;
And, in the auditoriums, conference centres and Billy Graham-
Rallying stadiums sometimes the atmosphere would be so
Charged with religious energies and wild spiritual abandon
That many mouths would start erupting into Tongues, splurging
Forth Glossolalia, the holy language of God, nonsensical
To human ears, apparently untranslatable, but somehow tapped
Spasmodically at such ecstatic gatherings, a deeply embedded
Babble, gabbling incomprehensibleness, whose otherworldly
Aural whorl made more reluctant Christians inwardly shudder,
Which seemed to release – or unleash – energies more primal
Than scriptural – Was this religion? Was this the oil of God?
The chemical of Christ? This hysterical crutch of faith… Was
Religious ecstasy supposed to be so psychically orgiastic –
Greased with Vaseline? Was religion the new orgasm? Rapture
Ectopically tapped far from erogenous zones – but from some

Pineal gland? Apostates felt instinctively that whatever this
Language was it wasn't God's – not the idiom of an Almighty,
But some argot of a demigod or demiurge, some strange and not
Altogether benign entity that magicked up this grotesque world
For metaphysical sport, a kind of trickster or sub-deity
Whose disobedience brought us forth; a rogue, rebellious spirit-*tóir*
That delighted in deceiving us into believing its' shibboleths
'Self-interest', 'privatisation', 'initiative', 'enterprise', 'competition',
'Individualism', 'free market', 'monetarism', and signing us up
To its warped perspectives (and what else was that antinomian
Evangelism but a spiritual Darwinism – Salvation
Of the fittest…?), Babel-babbles of the Big Bang unleashed
At the Stock Exchange in Nineteen Eighty-Six, the new torque
Tenets of history, torches of teleology, lighting the way
Into powerful shoulder-padded and sharp-elbowed futures,
The will to power, the triumph of the till over the depleting
Human spirit – and like all sinister minor gods, it tempted us
In deep-seeding whispers to reject compassion and philanthropy,
Embrace Capital and Property, *'dog eat dog'* over the underdog –
Exchange the mongrel of generosity for the pedigree of greed…

5

All the while the smoky pug-faced Old Labour god puffed his pipe
Disappointedly, purred ponderously, his large pale eyes
Drooping down, beleaguered by just how swift the swing from Left
To Right, in the blink of a milk-snatcher's eye, in terms of time;
How quick the dancing hands spread their palms then closed
Them tight again on their new gains and grasped still more
For whatever else, spiritual or material, was within their reach –
And soon the New Tongues, the strange Glossolalia
Of animal energies emitted indecipherable pheromones
Through every pore of politics, germinating in the new white heat
Of sharp collars and Paisley-patterned ties, compassion no longer
In fashion, Apache hair and corduroy flares scythed away
To layered styles and tapering chinos, gloss and gaudiness,
The new ergonomics for well-oiled ogres of self-gain;
A grab-it-all Bacchanalia of snatching bacilli overcame
The nation, a grasping plague, but there was no one to absorb
The blame, at least, not visibly, for this harsh and charmless abandon –
Those marginalised by the behavioural change got by on giros
And Mogadon, nostalgia for Nye Bevan, Bill Brand and Nigel Barton,
The socialist folk songs of Ewan MacColl, the polemical films
Of Potter, Loach, Brownlow and Mollo, Beta-blockers, Bleasedale's
Boys from the Blackstuff on Betamax, Seventies invective, Bennite
Tirades and glucose shots of Militant Tendency stomping off
The pinking Labour Party platform after being expelled for entry-
-ism, leaving behind them a sharp fizz like sherbet on the tongue;
Packet meals to placate rationed appetites, and, for some,
The occasional miracle of a charity hamper silently donated
On the doorstep by the more sympathetic fringe evangelists,
No wings attached, just cheap *Happy Shopper* haloes of budget-brand
Salvations with half-starved salivations and the tinned fruits
Of dialectical materialism arrested in syrups of acidic
Contradictions – and all the time more and more waxed avaricious,
Spoke in monetarist Tongues, of bartering, profiting, sculpting
Out opportunities from prisons of others' misfortunes,
Parasites of free enterprise; while those brought low by shifting
Attitudinal tides were ostracised by scraping plates of priorities
And consensuses; became microscopic anomalies in rock-pools
Of censuses, burrowed like sandworms into cloudy obscurity,

Strangers to Glossolalia's Golden Tongues and silver handshakes;
Classless skidders jolted out of place in the scheme of things,
Surpassed in status rapidly by blue collars now rinsed of bonds
And solidarity with fellow workers, homology hollowed out,
Common tongue decommissioned, allegiances deregulated,
Industries gutted, class-ties shredded in the grasp for mortgages –
Now socialism, the anathema, first casualty of the epidemic
Spiel of purely material *'aspiration'* sans cultivation, the mouse
Spun in a tangential wheel; those thrown to the bottom of the heap
Sucked on tinned substitutes of their labours' shrunken fruits,
A sour, metallic-tasting trickle-down of arrowroot,
As Tongues turned ingrown and swallowed themselves,
Strangling laryngeal angels, but liberating brutes…

Reading George Orwell's review of *Mein Kampf* at Liverpool Lime Street Station

25 January 2013

1

A biting day in January, the Liver Birds are frozen solid
On their high perches launched from neoclassical trunks
Scraping the mackerel sky, far above the gusty Mersey
And its chill, huddled docks, where one of my blackcoated
Ancestors worked as a shipping clerk in the early part
Of the twentieth century, spending what little spare time
He had craning by his Birkenhead desk-lamp translating
The Bible back into the Greek… I'm marching through the icy
Rains and sleety streets of winter Liverpool to Lime Street
Station's chilly vaulting, and the snowbound journey back
To the frostier South I'm not missing for a moment,
Charmed as I am by the classless Scouse welcoming – in spite
Of their drab habitat's inhospitable slippery pavements –
And that infectious accent that's a Lancashire hotchpotch
Sprinkled with Irish spice and a pinch of stewed Welshness,
Which – since the oral Diaspora of the Fifties' slum
Clearances – ricochets as far as Runcorn and Skelmersdale,
A kind of damp warmth, sharp-carved, Roman Catholic,
Clasped in against Anglican iciness, cushioned from
Its cold sculpted blasts by Flintshire's insulating hills…
The day after just one night in this priceless city, chorusing
Poetry at *The Bluecoat* – its icing-windowed court frozen
In the reign of obscure Queen Anne, last gasp of the Stuart clan
Before the Hanoverian rot set in – and a tub-thumping
Speech against this Torch-wielding Tory organ voluntary
Of a government – augmenting stigmatisation against
The disadvantaged, invalided and vulnerable swelling to full
Discriminating grind throughout public congregations
Summoned by blue blearing sirens of red-top fire engines
Screaming gutter-lies – to an audience of passionate
Lancastrians in an atmosphere of rare poetic commonality,

I pass a news-stand reading *FOUR YOUTHS BEAT HOMELESS MAN
TO DEATH*, while a street jazz band – as if in unconscious filmic
Percussion of tinny concussion – strikes up 'Singin' in the Rain',
And lurid images from Stanley Kubrick's Brutalist treatment
Of Anthony Burgess's dystopian *A Clockwork Orange*
(A psychopathic comic strip) intrude disturbingly in my mind:
The milk-drunk, bowler-hatted, cod-pieced Droogs sticking
Their canes and boots into the stomach of a wheezy old soused
Irish tramp in a litterless unreal subway – I'm reminded
Of the darker adumbrations of this austere time, where,
As the cascade of left-field literature reminds on its innumerable
Chewed spines in the tattered paper utopia of the *News from
Nowhere* bookshop, social scapegoats, folk devils and other
Shadow-projected grotesques of homespun mythologies
Promulgated by chalk-striped pigeon-men cooing in Whitehall
Corridors, now abound and balloon through hyperbolic red-tops
Along forked blue tongues, while the Bullingdon Boys put
The boot into the vulnerable, symbolically burning crisp fifty
Pound notes in front of the refrigerated eyes of rough sleepers…

2

Freezing over a cappuccino in icy Lime Street Station
Waiting for the train back to the snootier South, I thumb
My way through a cheap Prussian-grey stapled pamphlet
That might as well be contemporary, by old tobaccoy,
Equine-faced Eric Blair – aka George Orwell, hobo
Incognito for Mass Observation's silver-spooned invisibles –
Waging his war against gerunds and other rogue forms of prose-
Offenders, policing pretensions – and otherwise outsourcing
The moral conscience of his politicised times in spite of his
Faintly Hitlerish – or Chaplinesque – thin-trimmed toothbrush
Moustache and haircut (Forties' pudding-basin crop-top
With razor-short back and sides – a bit like Oswald Mosley) –
And snuck in at the back of the ten-a-penny dreadful,
His review of the unabridged *Mein Kampf*, from the *New
English Weekly*, 21st March Nineteen-Forty (I'm suddenly
Struck by the synchronicity of reading matter and station,
Those hoary rumours that a young Austrian *'artist'*,
Or jobless boho, Adolf H., once sojourned in Liverpool,
Avoiding the draft back in Vienna, boarding with his
Safety-razor businessman half-brother, the similarly
'Volatile' Alois, at his antagonistic digs in Toxteth,
From November 1912 to April 1913…): choicest
Polemical snippets strike me as I read: *'Both Left and Right
Concurred in the very shallow notion that National Socialism
Was merely a version of Conservatism'* – And, on wolfish
Adolf: *'A thing which strikes one is the rigidity of his mind';*
'Monomaniac'; George's recommended photograph: *'Hitler
In his early Brownshirt days. It is a pathetic, doglike face,
The face of a man suffering under intolerable wrongs. …'* –
At this junction I hollow out consumptive Orwell's long-
Drawn physiognomy, his ashy skin, his lipless mouth
Permanently chomping at a bit of polemical compromise,
A long horse-like *fizzog* with a stirrup-pinched grimace
(Though not as grossly proportioned as George Eliot's),
Not short of horse-sense, but groping for some composure
Between dialectically antagonistic tongs… Then I slip
Back to his Hitler depiction: *'The expression of innumerable
Pictures of Christ crucified… grievance against the universe…'*

(How Manichaean!); *'The martyr, the victim, Prometheus*
Chained to the rock… One feels, as with Napoleon, that he is
Fighting against Destiny, that he can't win, and yet that he
Somehow deserves to. The attraction of such a pose is quite
Enormous…' so George ploughs on in his unimpeachable prose…
And then the polemical uprooting of the phoney principle –
Or simply pragmatism?– of democracy (that is *rule by*
The people, *hoi demos*, at least, in theory, if not yet in practice,
And in that sense, little different to the long-projected hopes
Of still-unachieved Socialism, that milk-and-water-*ism*
They always say '*could never work*' – how convenient for them)
By comparison to the honest elemental self-harm,
General mayhem and bloodletting of Fascism, nonetheless,
To Orwell, '*psychologically far sounder than any hedonistic*
Conception of life' – I might agree with him on the matter
Of Capitalism, but depart at the notion of any '*soundness*'
To the jackboot swinging in, stamping on a human face;
While his flimsy shoehorning of Socialism as a politics
Which also states, as Capitalism does *sans* same shamed face,
'*I will offer you a good time*' (as opposed to a '*Good Time Coming*')
Sounds like the contra-talk of parrot-faced Peter Hitchens;
Did even lugubrious, iceberg-bound George unknowingly
Degrade language for propaganda purposes to prop up
His Aunt Sallies, keep his straw men upright in the '*pure wind*'?

3

I look out on the snow-flurried Liverpudlian night
At the scaly classical theatre opposite Lime Street Station,
Statically arced, petrol-patched like a baroquely camouflaged
Army tank, or a colossal stone armadillo about to pounce,
And wonder just how long it will be until another aggrieved,
Ghoulish, chip-shouldered 'upstart' grown from a damp pram
In a type of poverty deemed long obsolete by *'experts'* and *'tsars'*,
Humiliated, chronically pinched, unemployable, cramped
Up with cold like a mangy pigeon, nursing grudges like three-
Day's-growth, pacing grey streets tucked up in an army surplus
Trench-coat, too rigid, fired up and bloodcurdling of tongue
To fit in with those bohemians and college drop-outs
Who compose themselves with pianistic hands and twirl scarves
Effetely in thawing cafés of the Knowledge District,
Finds himself a platform or soapbox somewhere to tub-thump,
Ignite disgruntled audiences with ferocious oratory,
Mimetic, conductor-like gesticulations and chagrin-charging
Choreography – an epileptic Charlie Chaplin – turning
Bitter attentions to scapegoats in their vicinity, local, so more
Touchable, close at hand, observable, visible, a sub-species
Endangered simply by propinquity, easier to grasp
In the long-armed phalange, to tag with fiery turn-of-phrase,
Storming glares and armbands, scapegoats who in time are
Sculpted out from shadow-projected resentments, isolated
Through gallowglass looks, stigmatised then hounded to
The four corners of the city, and then, and there, this resurgent
Bulldog Breed finally finds its lead, its *'1930s moment'*,
The rise of a Unicorn incursion in some urban Uchronia curling
Towards a newer, grubbier reality in which everyone but
The ranting fanatical street apostle is the enemy, but none
More so than vermin, scurrying rats infesting every rusty-
Railinged basement squat, boarded-up digs, shut-curtained bed-sit,
Tipped out from their slumming burrows and poured out with
Their soupy shadows into pounding precincts, sunlight-disinfected,
Rounded up, culled, pinned with little blue stars or black triangles,
Paraded up and down the pavements to the fascist laughter
Of mercilessly innocent children; a time of spit-and-polishing,
Frothing and dribbling, boot-trampling platitudes, ghetto-

Rhetoric, doughnut-dialectic, and social cleansing sugared
As *'gentrification'* (or *'purification'*, *'fumigation'*), a tramping
Of hope and protections, the clinching of a pincer-movement
On the poor, the unemployed, preoccupied and stupefied,
Mushrooming spontaneously with toadstools, pop-up soup
Kitchens and ten-a-penny food banks, for only that way can
This damaged, aggrieved pariah, this scowling, wolfish, frothing-
Mouthed natural victim fulfil his twisted motto: *'Better an end*
With horror than a horror without end' – and only unsolicited
Poets and neurotics to spot it, stop it, protest, or pretend
That none of it is happening, or is just a passing trend
Which will wring its' usage out just like a struggling gerund…

Orwell Mansions

Green & Pleasant, Shiny & New, Life & Soul –
Glossy slogans of Catalyst Housing's gentrification of Golborne:
New ergonomically gracious and spacious penthouse suites,
Duplexes and precincts springing up rapidly around newly
Named Portobello Square, formerly Wormington Green,
Where two new-build luxury apartment blocks are almost complete,
One called Hardy Mansions, replete with its own ground-floor plaza,
Shops and salubrious boutiques, *pour une nation de boutiquiers*
(Though today, in lieu of Good Samaritans, it's more a case
Of *'No room at the Inn'*, the British now the Brutish, not so
Much a nation of shopkeepers as innkeepers), lush greeneries
Margining the concourse as piloted at Lillie Square's grime-free
Gardened cloisters, cool roomy chandeliered lobbies for
The City boys, and, in propinquity to unspoken protocols
Of *'poor doors'*, portals to opposite worlds of ill-gotten luxury
And affordable poverty, segregated by the girths of buildings:
One door for the rich, one for the poor; metal studs on the concrete,
Under the porch-ways of course (to repel the human pigeons
That try to nest there by night) – Ah! Nostalgia for those down-
And-out days when one could always find a dark patch
In which to get one's bonce down – not so today: if gaunt
George Orwell, the Observation Hobo, was to try and lie down
On one of those beds of metal studs he'd get a rude awakening
All right, a spike straight *up that place where the sun don't shine!
Not a hand up, but a spike up!* to readapt the pull-them-up-by-
Their-boot-straps *Big Issue* red-top-appeasing strapline)…
The other nondescript complex is called – *sans* hint of dystopian
Quip – Orwell Mansions, although Catalyst Housing (located in
A blue portacabin on Ladbroke Grove) are never knowingly
Undersold on irony; while one can be sure that the revenant
Namesake of the estate's purely serendipitous eponym
Will be chuckling to himself while thumbing through the slippery
Catalyst Housing brochure, perusing their expansive portfolio,
Reeling at corporate copy overgrown with neologisms
And gerunds as he goes, wondering how Gordon Comstock –

Had he actually existed outside the author's warping
Imagination – would have negotiated such unattractive
Nomenclature into his advertising copy, how he'd have
Couched them in his prefabricated prose primed to interpolate
Spending habits, persuade consumers to shop for commodities
Produced by the Company that employed his supremely
Commercial Muse, his nose for an eye-catching phrase, world-
Beating trope, with pecuniary Compliments; thumping out his
Unimpeachable spiel in the white plush and potted aspidistras
Of an impersonal copywriting suite – breaking off at 1pm prompt
For a spot of coffee-fetishism: Starbucks' insipid beige soup,
And one of many multicoloured cupcakes, ubiquitous sugar-
Rush comestibles of pristine indistinguishable cafés
All a-whir with grinding beans, acrobatic baristas, wireless signals
And gossiping solipsists plugged into hands-free phones,
i-pods, i-pads, wi-fi, Blackberries, tablets, and impossibly compact
Micro-books where friends, relatives and lovers are reduced
To touch-screen pixies, pixelated Lilliputians, who, however,
From their own views, are enlarged Gullivers vicariously
Travelling through cloudscapes of Skype, until such time
As the machine stops its' macro-mollycoddling – so many weird
And wonderful means of communication so human beings
Can keep interacting at comfortable distances without having
To leave comfort zones, now even conversation can be
Conducted by proxy, personality deputed, and anyone
Can join in with tangential threads, or, provided they're pithy,
The synthetic titbits of Twitter – though with such abundance
Of contact mediums, communication seems to contract,
There seems less urgency for rapid responses, acknowledging
Messages, as if we share some mediumship of emailing
Telepathically wired-in, cross-circuited clairaudience;
After all, virtual conversation is just one remove from solipsism;
Orwell's ghost harangues the rogue gerunds of hashtag messages
While furiously sipping at his ever-depleting, tantalising
Flat white, delectably tasteless substance, as from his glassy vantage-
Point craning over an ever-receding coffee-table on the ever-
Plunging precipice of a brown leather couch, he grouchily
Apprehends his ergonomic legacy – not in the warping spines
Of overripe polemics and polished dystopian prose, nor in

The glaring angular visage of a triangular residential wedge
Registered under his *nom de plume*; and as caliginous Arabic
Beans imbue their phantasmagorical gradualist effects,
Percolating his endorphins, he imagines himself as Howard
Carter discarnate gazing at a half-submerged pyramid,
His fingers twitching with anticipation at discovering Tutankhamun's
Other tomb, his fugitive crypt – but it's not a trowel he grips,
Just a cartridge pen, one of the many writing artefacts buried
With him – a dust-bloomed typewriter weighing down the lid
Of his glass sarcophagus inside its' flat-packed pyramid…

New Era

Built as affordable flats in the mid-1930s,
Knee-deep in the Great Depression, under the black-capped
Government of Jackdaw Baldwin, Old Austerity Stan,
A square of tall-windowed blocks of bricks in ochres
And browns... Today, in the *'Great Recession'* of the mid-
Twenty Teens, the now old 'New Era', in Hoxton,
Has passed into the hands of Westbrook Partners Consortium
Of the US, and then into the grubby mitts of the Benyon
Estate, co-owned by an eponymous Tory MP, only for
A last-minute *'goodwill gesture'* from said company
By pulling out from its stake in the investment; now,
Back to Westbrook again, the baton passes on in a 'return'-
Thirsty relay race: in spite of Philip Glanville and Hackney
Council's urging of both Benyon and Westbrook
Not to increase rents on New Era to market rates,
As per the gentlemen's agreement that the rents wouldn't rise
Until Twenty-Sixteen, the Council has been reliably informed
By Westbrook – listed already as a *'predatory landlord'*:
'Since this week's departure of the Benyon Estate we understand...
That Westbrook no longer plans to honour that plan, and have been
Told that their plan is to refurbish the current estate in its entirety
And then rent out all the properties without secure tenancies
At market rates, with no affordable housing' – effectively
This means that the current residents will likely be evicted
Before the year is out, gentrified just in time for Christmas,
And packed off into B&Bs, hostels, or tipped onto the streets;
Rent promise rescinded, now it's over to Hoxton Regeneration
Ltd to sort out protocols and manoeuvres then sweep up –
Or, a more appropriate metaphor, 'mop up' – afterwards,
Refurbish the flats in time for a newly minted generation
Of flusher residents – for this new era's gentrification...

[*Stop press:* important not to prematurely despair:
A last ditch deal between Westbrook and Dolphin Square,
A charitable foundation, which has bought up New Era
And thereby, for the time being, kept the tenants there –
A fountain of promise springs up from Dolphin Square…
And bang on the New Year, Saturday 31st
Of January 2015, the people stomp the capital
In their March for Homes, and a giant banner's hung
On Tower Bridge demanding: *'Social Housing
Not Social Cleansing'* – a show of people power;
But a bit too late for gentrified Balfron Tower…
And, elsewhere, everywhere, the Big Smoke is busy
Being gentrified: Butterfields E17 has just bought up
Some social housing stock, tenants protesting prompt
At impending eviction without consultation – while
Plans are afoot to stifle Bunhill Fields with scaffolding,
Blot out Blake's gravestone in ink-shadows of buildings,
But we can be sure they'll be building no Jerusalem,
Just more tower blocks in Beelzebub's bejewelled jerry-slum…].

Eton Mess

O what an Eton Mess they've made
And the trouble with an Eton Mess
Is it's left to those who didn't indulge
To clear it all up, we're afraid

'Two parties coming together to clear up the mess left by
Another' – that's *Labour*, in case the mantra didn't
Quite register: that's what the Tories said when they
Scraped back into power on the back of a Faustian
Fag-pact with the Liberal Orange Book Brigade –
But in place of that *'mess'*, which was, in any case,
In the process of being mopped up, the Tories
Concocted their own choicest Etonian equivalent:
Strawberries and cream for the ruling Falange,
While the poor were crushed up to bits of meringue…

O what an Eton Mess they've made
But the trouble with an Eton Mess
Is it's left to us to clear it up, we're afraid

It certainly isn't a *'mess'* that these ministers
Inherited from privileged parents, but multi-
Million pound estates and investments, not least
The prime minister, born with a gold-plated spoon
In his chops, weaned by a stockbroker father
Whose tax contributions were bountifully delayed –
Or cryogenically frozen – via Switzerland,
And Panama, amassing a handsome fortune
Through which his son was furnished a warmed-up place
At Eton, then Brasenose, Oxford, and a catapult
Up into PR with a reference from his fifth cousin,
Elizabeth Saxe-Coburg-Gotha (Windsor) Regina –
So much for meritocracy, Equal Opportunities:
Now positive discrimination is upside-down,
No embarrassment of riches these days, no

Apologies for privileges, no taboos in obscene
Displays of conspicuous consumption – now is
The empurpled patch of open-palmed nepotism…

O what an Eton Mess they've made
But the trouble with an Eton Mess
Is it's left to us clear it up, we're afraid

These Etonian Tories said they'd *'Make Work Pay'*,
But we didn't realise they meant they'd make
The *workers pay to work* through wage freezes,
And the unemployed pay through benefit caps
Fraying fabrics of claimants forced into workfare
Placements packing *Poundland* stores, fobbed off
With sub-minimum wages – *ARBEIT*
McMACHT MITT FRIES! And when they said
'We're all in this together', we didn't realise they
Simply meant themselves as a separate species,
While we were left *'in it'* – the *merde*; sealed in
Their impunity from effects of Their *'difficult decisions'*,
'Tough choices' and cuts inflicted on the rest of *Us*…

O what an Eton Mess they've made
But the trouble with an Eton Mess
Is it's left to us to clear it up, we're afraid

O the Tories have certainly made an Eton Mess
Of our demotic tongue, turned words on their heads:
Whipping up dysphemisms of hatred towards
Their impoverished victims: the unemployed,
Now *'skivers'* as opposed to *'strivers'*, helped by
Red toppings of glacier cherries on firmaments
Of spoon-fed cream and meringue, finger-spongers
And 'Scroungermongering'; they've all but scooped
Out common phrases of their true ingredients
And replaced them with synthetic substitutes:
'Do the right thing', *'Roll up our sleeves'*, *'Something for*
Nothing', and some faint notion they confuse as
'Fairness' – the list goes on and gets more nauseating

The more mouthfuls one has to swallow; now *'fit
For work'* is dished out to those who are fit to drop –
As many soon do within just six weeks of being
Stripped of support for their sicknesses – so stalks
The Atos Albatross: Lazarus gets up and limps
Over the precipice of suicides and unreported
Deaths buried with statistics until finally surfacing
To confirm the departure of 91,000-plus souls –
While ex-Remployees are 'liberated' onto doles,
Stripped of dignity – no opt-outs with Digintas…

*O what an Eton Mess they've made
But the trouble with an Eton Mess
Is it's left to us to clear it up, we're afraid*

Five years into elective and selective austerity
For the poorest, tax breaks for the rich, amid all this
Conspicuous under-consumption, supermarket
Shelves display fashionable dishes: Pulled Pork (as if
To mimic the dismembering of our social fabric
By porcine speculators) with a side dish
Of Rumbledethumps (potato, cauliflower,
Cabbage, all thrown in together); followed by
A choice of desserts: Salted Caramels in the shape
Of paper envelopes delivering verdicts from
The Department of Whipping and Puddings, Customer
Compliance-sprinkled toppings without proper tasting
Trials, spiced with a bite, and bitter manila
Aftertaste; or the ubiquitous luxury dessert,
Eton Mess, available in various interpretations,
But all with a thick upper-crust of meringue pieces…

*O what an Eton Mess they've made
But the trouble with an Eton Mess
Is it's left to us to clear it up, we're afraid*

How did this strange melange of a pudding begin?
Apparently its riotous concoction was an accident –
As with so many traditions – but no serendipity:

It happened in the eponymous school's 'sock shop'
('Tuck' to us Commoners) during the Thirties
(So fitting its modern revival in our repeat-run
Of that unevenly fleeced decade, under the most
Right-wing government since Stanley Baldwin's –
Neville Chamberlain, Dr Crippen to Stafford Cripps'
Mr. Kipling); originally made with strawberries or
Bananas mingled with cream, and dredged together,
While the meringue was added to the deluge later –
So Eton Mess is actually a mashed-up Pavlova!
The Barbarian British equivalent to the elegant
Dessert of the Ballet Russe – brass instead of silver;
Our Etonian elites relish a mess, and, not unlike
The Russians – who throw their finished Vodka
Glasses over their shoulders to hiss in fireplaces –
Love nothing better than the sound of breaking glass!

O what an Eton Mess they've made
But the trouble with an Eton Mess
Is it's left to us to clear it up, we're afraid

A gooey fug of ingredients, this Eton Mess:
A slush-up of the public sector, NHS
And welfare state to cherry-picked pinkish
Privatised cream, strawberries asset-stripped,
Free of flavour at the point of spivery;
And as for the wealth gap, yolk separated,
Its egg-white's whipped up into an inflated
Meringue of vast girth that spirals up to
A curled peak so high it's invisibly blue…

As for the class divide, well that's another story
In terms of desserts: more a Knickerbockerglory…

O what an Eton…. Etc.

Coventry Blue

'And though his hue
Be not Coventrie-blue
Yet he is undone
By the threade he has spunne.'
Ben Jonson, *The Masque of Owles*

1

They say that true blue means to stay fast and true
However antediluvian the view –
It's those who don't waver: Covenanters,
Conservatives, and all other Naysayers;

The phrase was rinsed from another phrase,
As many are, wrung through human gaze,
Then pressed in the mangle of the rolling tongue:
'As true as Coventry Blue' – and John Ray's

Compleat English Proverbs traced its root
To a cloth whose fibres were so resolute
That it lost none of its colour when washed,
As stubborn as obstructed blood going bruit;

This cloth was manufactured in Coventry
And was dyed a deep blue most commonly,
A blue fast and true that became *'true blue'*:
'Always the same and like himself' – verily

Unwavering views – this *'Coventry'* Blue
Came to emblemise blue through and through,
To remain fast, steadfast, intransigent
To the last; obdurate; not to be moved –

Not to be moved by abject poverties
Of corn-famished murmurs and reaper pleas,
But resist Progress, pettifog Reform –
The future can't leapfrog if kept on its knees...

2

True to vested views, whether true or untrue –
Anything is true if repeated until *'blue
In the face'* – for the clothier, dyer and Tory
Are *'always the same'* and themselves, those who

Can afford to stay true to false truths, steadfast
In the din of Siren change, lashed to the mast,
Or fixed to the post as scarecrows in a sough
Stuffed thick with burnt straw of waterproof Past –

Damp straw of Tradition: a cornucopia
For those big with gain, ripe utopia
Spilt from the plenty of falsely split grain:
The chaff is scythed off for the sunburnt thresher,

While blooms of spent profits speckle brown fields
Like Duke Blue of cornflowers: bond yields
For absent landlords, mirage-rewards
For workers: blue smudges to work towards;

Though it seems remoter the more it grows
In blossom promise, the old blue rose,
The something blue of *noblesse oblige*,
The something borrowed of labour by liege…

3

The rich sup ripe apples while the pipped peasants
Are chucked sour cores of antidepressants
To sharpen up penury-depleted spirits –
Or prodded with shocks of Protestant Ethics;

Tradition is the curd of recurring decline,
Bad habits of the past marbleised; a shrine
To Going prolonged – Age's glazed scagliola;
Green- and blue-veined as a turgid gorgonzola,

Varicose, carious, congealed against change;
Ingrained allergic gesture, glorious mange
Of Time's glassed intransigents, blue bloom grown
From mould of human tragedies in air-tight dome;

An acquired Danish Blue of Establishment,
Odorous of old socks and musty parchment:
Past on repeat – Society-in-a-rut:
One long rigged re-enactment by the Sealed Knot;

English democracy, a paper mummery
Of rags and tatters, parliamentary
Music hall vaudeville raising the rafters
To drown out the toc-toc of partitioned grafters

Hatching from lobbying grubs behind panels
In woodloused shadows, harvesting channels
And burrows of power borrowed by us
From suffrage-adjustors: *domine, dirige nos* –

The Speaker polices the pitch of debate
At just the right decibel so as to conflate
With the scuttling of the *Commons Rhinomacer*,
One eye to the prompt-boxed Remembrancer…

4

History's a lottery of long and short straws:
The latening harvests of a travestied poor
Upstaged by gold sheaves of the privileged few,
Tall narratives writ by the makers of Law –

But the chronicling rich are occasionally
Deceived by depictions in parsimony,
Their versions of events, *their* ancestor-worship,
Their rose-tinted past, more oftener rosehip –

And that's the strange thing about nostalgia:
A part-longing for things that never were,
So iron resolves to return us to some
Green English idyll, are wrought with danger,

As they were with the prim shopkeeper's daughter
From Grantham, Margaret Hilda Thatcher,
Who strove to re-cultivate Victorian values,
Acquisitiveness, avarice: captive virtues;

She described herself as a *'true blue'* Tory,
Decreed there was *'no such thing as society'*,
Only individuals, self-help, transaction –
And those who protested were sent to Coventry:

The red rose of English socialism
Is still wilting there in that tight-lipped prison
Of stiff Britishness, but for a change of heart –
Too late for blue blazers and blue-rinse women;

Ever more visible through English skins
Veins blush bluer now, some empurpling
With rush of impressionable blood bamboozled
By a pincer-movement of Prelapsarian

Campaigns which point to the same false premise
On the map as to when the so-called Lapse
Actually happened, marking the spot
That for yesterday's ragged improved their lot

Substantially for the first time in history:
The Attlee Settlement towards equality;
But Purple tub-thumpers are attempting today
To wind back the clocks multi-culturally,

Turn round the *Windrush*, whip up the tailwinds
That pump the rubicons of white haemoglobins,
'NO ROMA' euphemised as *'No Romanians'*;
Repatriate powers from Flemish mandarins,

Blimp out from the European experiment
In human rights and employment protections…
The other campaign, in wrecking-ball swing
For four years of an Eton Blue Government

Has managed to do more vandalising
Of social democracy than managed during
Eighteen hatchet years of Thatcherism:
Having dismantled almost everything

That was worth preserving, the last vestiges
Of the Welfare State and the NHS,
Supplanting them with food banks, zero-hours
Contracts, mandatory unpaid work placements;

These Eton Blues have almost reconstructed
The shabby rich-poor chic of Thirties' rusted
Cultural sclerosis – now Tories no more staid,
But retro, coolly out of touch, almost trusted,

In spite of their *'SO-last-century'* template
Of the National Government of post-Wall Street
Crash austerity under the hawk-like wing
Of Means Test-and-labour camp Stanley Baldwin…

5

We're hurtling back to the Thirties today
In our Eton Blue Twenty-First Century –
Our leaders once more cut from public school cloths,
Abetted by Liberal buff-coloured moths;

Those shop steward days of woodbines and roses,
Of scholarship Harolds, Teds, Jameses – oases
Of opportunity for more life-shaped opinions
Cropped amid landscapes of palmed nepotisms;

Empirical pools slowly emptied to glimmerings
Of once-greening gains, while privileged springs
Gush back with blue vengeance – in hindsight, a mirage,
That gentler interregnum of grammar and marge

And lowering rungs, when Meritocracy's rise
Was more than just a glint in Michael Young's eyes,
But already rooting, up until it was nipped
In its proleptic bud when the Milk Snatcher quipped

She'd *'banish the dark, divisive clouds of Marxist
Socialism'* – as she did, promptly replacing it
With the dark, divisive clouds of private avarice,
Of property-worship and acquisitiveness,

Pub-emptying pulls for blue collars, carrots
And sticks: Right-to-Buys and Buy-to-Lets;
(Young Junior mapped – while his father was napping –
Playgrounds that trapped the sound of no hands clapping)…

Parliamentary parties since embraced her Creed
Of venerable envy and respectable greed,
Once opposite stripes of Metropolitan elites
Now at cross purposes as how best to pleat

The Emperors' Patched-Up Clothes of Capitalism,
Each myopic Minister trimming with precision
The pinking fabric of imperceptible schism,
Flipside apparels, Chippings/Primrosians,

Snipped from the same auspicious cloth; cut a dash
In pinstripes from shadbellies, bespoke catercaps;
The propertied prosper in spite of the Crash,
Capitalise on it to barbarically slash

The public purse and safety nets for the poorest,
Pull up the drawbridge, slam down the portcullis;
Westminster's rentiers all quids in together
While the rest of us are sent to Coventry forever…

6

It's true that blue is back with a vengeance,
Eton, Oxford, Cambridge blues, nuances
Of this most misappropriated of pigments
(Azure in Bluemantles' heraldic parlance);

To think that the tincture of sky and sea
Should be wine-darkened with reactionary
Stains, be used as a rinse for prejudice,
And a dye for pedigreed embroideries

The purpose to which Coventry Blue
Was mostly put, Royal and Windsor Blue,
For the purple-blooded rulers in hues
Of Blue Dominions and domino blooms

Championed by rosettes of Tory Blue,
And once by the Buff and Blue Whigs: two
Sides of the same Royal Mint, one for
The Stuarts, the other for Hanover

In days before more progressive Whigs
Re-branded as Liberals – Herbert Asquith's
Government, their crowning achievement came with
Chancellor Lloyd George's *'People's Budget'*

Which, in laymen's terms, did a Robin Hood:
Robbed from the rich for the common good;
New alms for the unemployed – after all
The rich were not rich through effort but gall

Of land-grabbing robber baron ancestors,
Their properties entrusted from speculators;
The *'Welsh Wizard'* waved his wand, wishing to see
Poverty become as remote in this country

'As the wolves which once infested its forests';
And this '*dole*', though swiftly denigrated as
'*Going on the Lloyd George*', promised that
Before long those wolves would nearly vanish,

But through another party which represented
The common people, thus feared, resented,
Transgressors of the messengers but keepers
Of their message, and of their sisters and brothers

In cooperative fellowship: Labour campaigned
Under a blood-crimson banner, arraigned
Privileged legislators of suffrage's grains,
Harangued the well-to-do for ill-gotten gains

And made establishments tremble at their
Green rosettes (perhaps after the Levellers'
Sea-green ribbons) – then blanch York-white
At the change to the Red Rose of Lancaster…

7

But Labour's first taste of government, blighted
By the Wall Street Crash – the party alighted
Into Opposition when its' leader, prime
Minister James Ramsay MacDonald ignited

Its' anger at the pronouncement of a cut
In unemployment benefit due to the rut
Of recession – its' leader decapitated
From its' trunk for having capitulated

To right-wing guillotining of the meagre
Grains for indigents, first savage eagre
To bash at the decks of the workless – Arthur
Henderson in place as the party's new leader;

MacDonald clung onto to his premiership,
Head of a National Government, a ship
Groaning with Tories and Liberals – True Blues
And Blue and Buffs…After a catastrophic

Second World War, the result of a decade
Of Depression and austerity that frayed
The very nervous fabric of the Continent
And erupted into panic and Fascist vent,

Labour won a landslide election victory
In spite of Winston's oratory, the Tory
Way was not for a time of peace: under Clement
Attlee, construction started on a Settlement

Of level ground, a new Social Contract,
The Welfare State, wolfless forests made fact,
And though the aim now was full employment,
A thorough National Assistance Act

Was introduced to serve as a safety net in case
Of recessions ahead – while in order to efface
The social diseases of rickets and *'white plague'*,
Nye Bevan ushered in a National Health Service

Free at the point of use, free prescriptions
In place of private doctors' fee proscriptions
For the poorest, now all could access treatment
'From cradle to grave', no matter their stations,

And in accordance with this embryonic
New Jerusalem, dispensation of a tonic
Called Socialism, albeit in small doses
Of ration books laced with essence of red roses;

A social oasis of six years saw Beveridge's
Five Giant Evils – *'Want, Ignorance, Idleness,
Disease and Squalor'* – subjugated; and with this
New age came heartfelt and mindful changes,

A burgeoning hunger for grasping higher things
Than the soul-destroying rote of earning livings –
Now people had energy to regain insights long
Lost to foraging now they had full bread-bins,

And feed an indescribable craving inside them
For something immaterial, soul-nourishing,
Some manna for the mind, an inedible thing:
Knowledge, so filling, yet tasting of nothing…

8

Now was ushered in an age of sky-blue grace
When, for three decades, that purple trace
Rinsed fainter and fainter, and pale blue
Pelicans occupied polemical space,

Richly instructive but cheaply priced
At sixpence a pinch, pocket-sized
Paperback manna: reimbursement
In trickledown tri-band bouleversement;

Blue-and-white thrift titles to the put-upon
Proletariat, now lifted up on
Pinions of social philosophy,
Purchased and trousered philanthropy –

Ripe pickings for black-nailed autodidacts,
The real life Jude Fawleys, Frank Owens, bracts
Of the artisan class whose sepals support
The mortarboard petals of the middling sort,

But whose own thirst for didactic succour,
So long neglected as wrinkle and pucker
In cloth cut for donkey work, multiplied
To corduroyed ridges that couldn't be dyed

In the usual adulterated yellow-rinse
Of sports colours, gossip, prurience
Scooped up by Grub Street's bowdlerising hacks,
Racing tips feathering their bowler-hats;

This corduroy was no newfangled fabric,
It was an ancient cloth of an authentic
Shade gained with age, and its' furrowed textures
Demanded nourishment, a cut of ploughshares –

So it fell to red hearts of the better-heeled
To redistribute to them belated bond yields:
Budget-brand books for workers downed tools
To browse as they put up their feet slipped in mules;

Portable libraries of pale-blue spines
Well worth the swop of a pint or some woodbines,
Rows upon rows for browsing and thumbing,
Accessible blues of ambrosial plumbing;

Each in its striped livery, colour-coded
By subject: dark blue for biographies, red
For drama, sky-blue for social sciences,
Cerise for travel, purple for belles-lettres,

And those sea-green intrigues (less encouraged),
Crime fiction a cut above colportage
Potboilers – common folk's cultural cures,
Wholesome brown stouts of yeasty literatures…

A toast to these cheap jewels of *Woolworths*,
These thrupence Promethean sprinklings
Composed by sympathetic public school-
Tailored Bluecoats and bluestockings,

But also by some brought up to abuses
Of slum-dwelling: Richard Hoggart's *The Uses
Of Literacy*; thus an educational
Cross-class exchange generated – fruitful

Tariffs showered on *hoi polloi* shoppers,
The paper fruits of affordable knowledge,
Price of a packet of fags, to refurbish
Each slum as a sociological college;

Primers for blue-collar scholarship,
Scraps for black-coated Pooters to catch up
On a spot of self-improvement – or for
The rackety self-taught schoolmaster

To swot up on up-to-date arguments
And charge up his pupils with supplements,
Skip round the classroom with sparkling craw,
A beak-full of pearls, a black-caped jackdaw…

But those sky-blue days when acquisition
Of knowledge to nourish minds was a mission
Of the masses under the egalitarian
Aegis of progressive tortoise-shelled men

Collapsed long ago with the last pit-splint,
Abruptly replaced by the philistine mint:
Commodity-fetishism, conspicuous
Consumption, visceral acquisitiveness

For the purely material – the unsympathetic
Magic of capitalism's confidence trick
Pricks all but consciences; business is business,
And blue-sky thinking has Coventry blueness…

9

But what was the secret of that ineffaceable
Coventry cloth? Was its blue dyed-in-the-wool?
Or was the cloth dipped in blue dye afterwards?
Whatever way round, the blue's immovable,

Just as it is in blue-bruising British eyes,
Blues that can't stain, stubborn island dyes
Persist the more they're rinsed, can never be
Washed out, no matter how hard the rain tries;

This race has its green and red ephemerals,
A thin seam of sea-green germinal
Remaining diminishingly – but purples
And blues are our hardiest perennials:

No English shades are so doggedly engrained
In our island mind, so permanently stained
In our cultural fabric as these princely hues,
Emperors of the spectrum: purples and blues –

Sovereign regents in the primogeniture
Of English pigments, entitled tinctures:
Which, when mingled, congeal into Crown-
Rinse of the Aristocracy of Colours:

Coventry Blue – so resolute, so true
'To itself and always the same', through and through,
Impermeable, inscrutable blue,
Ineluctable Baron of British rubes;

Our island race prizes above anything
The right to self-determination,
The right to be told to *'do the right thing'*,
The right to take flight on just the right wing;

The right to be ruled by those who know best
What is and is not *'in the national interest'*;
The right to have opinions spoon fed us
By red-top parrots with blue-torch crests;

The right to worship at the planted feet
Of the elephant god of property –
Ganesha of buy-to-letting agencies;
The right to fleece tenants through legalese;

The right to buy up unlimited empties;
The right to deny others' rights to tenancies:
'No smokers. No children. No Chavs. No pets.
No unemployed mothers. No benefits';

The right to earn livings to cover the rent
For castles which we've no entitlement
To enter; the right to elective enslavement,
Grey subservience we revel in: employment;

Britons may *'never, never, never… be slaves'*
But will ever be servants; reeves of grey waves;
Our green island salvage is a gem of mildew
In a sea not of silver but Coventry Blue…

**Tan
Raptures**

The Decision-Makers: A Coventry Story

i.m. Mark and Helen Mullins

> 'Coventry is going to be a people's city, where people believe that
> human life can be good, and pleasant. It will not be every one
> for himself, but everyone for the good and happiness of all
> people living. Every man will believe in that goal and the
> happiness that is to be shared – to be shared equally.'
> Dylan Thomas, 'A City Reborn'

> 'And now cold charity's unwelcome dole
> Was insufficient to support the pair;
> And they would perish rather than would bear
> The law's stern slavery, and the insolent stare
> With which law loves to rend the poor man's soul –
> The bitter scorn, the spirit-sinking noise
> Of heartless mirth which women, men, and boys
> Wake in this scene of legal misery.'
> Shelley, 'A Tale of Society as it is: From Facts, 1811'

1

Necessity sent them twelve miles once a week from out
In the sticks to Coventry's alfresco concrete archipelagos
Of soup kitchens to stock up on vegetables for the next six
Days' simmering; hotchpotch Scotch broth's thermal winter
Warmer – the empty stomach's nauseous thaumaturgy –
Acidy on the tongue as rosehip, punctuated by
The prosaic Eucharist of cheap tin loaf – to insulate
Their blood through cold-cutting months in damp warrens
Of a three-quarters' unheated house, nestled in the Hobbit-
Hutch of the one warm room where a rust-corrupted
Radiator would hold court to its' huddled subjects;
A burrow of warped rugs, torn covers; a cushioned den
Turreted by a curved-spined settee… But for all the parsnip
Soup and twice-sliced white, simply to survive wasn't enough
Reason to live, not worth the endurance, in the end;

The diminishing dignities of obscurely thriving poverties;
The poorly phrased Appeal letters stating recondite *'reasons'* –
Byzantine as patterns on shells of molluscs clinging
To soggy morsels of ominous brown envelopes unpeeling
On the doorstep in automatic mornings: impersonal
Lines detailing arbitrary *'decisions'* as to why no benefits
Would be forthcoming in spite of incapacities chronic
As the black symbolic damp patch on the toilet's melting ceiling,
Slowly bruising with signs of encroaching outsides – faith
Dwindling; brutal white tribunal papers stubbornly refusing
To transubstantiate into something more nourishing
Than mould of inedible typeface, morsels of spores resistant
To repealing, darkly alchemical… Unleavened, then; leaden,
Their shadow-scoured faces – until a glacial acquiescence
To extinction overcame them – or him: practical protector,
Carer, keeper, interpreter for his remedial familiar
Dismissed by DWP mandarins for being incapable
Of catching abstruse questions' darting arrows aimed at her
Inarticulate target, couched in equivocating quivers, barrels
Of verbal apples her brow was somehow supposed to balance –
Which made her husband's bowing fingers twitch like William
Tell's… She, then, deemed unfit to qualify as unfit for some
Occulted hectoring thing called *'Work'*, ghettoised outside
The point-score system of people-sieving (no room for human
Flourishing amongst tight-fisted flowers of welfare-sifting,
Only the agony-nourishing of gut-churning sanctions)…

2

She, considered too cognitively ill-equipped to vouch for her
Incapacity: illiterate, innumerate, thus ineligible
For *'signing on'*, her signature illegible, her cowering brow,
Unintelligible as a stumped Munchkin's – a shadow's no
Recourse to claim assistance from the light: no more are benefits
An inalienable birthright for Britishers denied the right
To work in ineffectively *'competitive'* employment markets –
That safety-net fit for catching unskilled heroes, fundamental
Rights for which our grandparents and great-grandparents
Fought, and finally won, through the long plough of war,
As an acknowledgement for their mass sacrifice towards
The defeat of fascism and in defence of our nation from
Its interference (only to inherit an inland fiscal equivalent);
Rudimentary entitlements to state assistance covenanted
In Clement Attlee's Emerald City Settlement, now, in this
Latter-day Thirties' restoration, of empty plates, soup-coupons,
Sanctioning, rationing and moth-eaten *KEEP SCHTUM AND
CARRY ON* legends, all rattled back to scraps by pinstriped
Apostles of another impostor *'Wizard of Aus'*, the glacial
Iain Duncan Smith and his welfare reform henchman,
And fellow Mendelist, 'Lord' Freud of Schadenfreude,
He of the brutal trope on empathising with the unemployed:
'You don't have to be the corpse to go to the funeral'; even for
The unemployable soul, the most occupationally *un-
Pigeonhole-able*… Not so for Mrs Mullins, a blunt thorn in linen-
Suited sides of serge-skinned Social Hygienists at Customer
Compliance ruminating on mentholated bones
Of anthropomorphic polo mints… *'So…'* (that fashionable
Adverb that starts so many replies today, designed to sideline
Questions, outsource answers, cloud transparencies
Of culpabilities to wilful blindness)… scooped of state support
To social insecurities, so… implicitly stripped of spiritual
Citizenship – penalised from the *'species essence'* – for the 'sin':
Uneconomic; chronic as an unproductive cough; a poltergeist
In the small-print; a benign incubus in tick boxes' pinched
Squares of passport benefits and their knock-on domino
Effects subliminally navigated by novice clairvoyants,
Boatfuls of bemused Bermudas; Mrs Mullins, a ghost with

A child's intelligence quotient, projected on a magic carpet
Cut to fit the Big Cloth-Eared Society that shrinks more
Every minute; an after-echo from halcyon days of lean-to
Privations, food dockets, parish alms, poor relief, lip-paid doles
(*Doules* for debt-slaves), Salvation Army vanguards serving
And converting soupy vagrants to baptismal inner-cleansings…
She, a throwback to those long-gloomed times before
People's Budgets, Beveridge Reports and nimbly assembling
Welfare states, presently dismantling to post-aborted
Shadows of good intentions, granulated gradualisms…

3

These two cloudy specimens had, as the worn idiom goes,
'Slipped through the net' of withering safeties... Their unfussy
Suicide, a psychic de-cluttering, a study in unforthcoming
Clichés of innocence disposed expediently, with minimum
Stain on the state's tarnishing, nor so much as a tacit
Accusation of moral bankruptcy of powers that be
And do as they wouldn't be done by... An open verdict
Cavalierly recorded by cheddary gnarled magistrates,
Glibly absorbed, then flippantly passed with the port,
Strictly to the Right, at Pontius Pilate's table in the Chancellery...
A fungus of factors contributed – *of course, of course* – not one
Single identifiable thing: it was a culmination;
A crop of dry-rot descriptors and blue mould accruing;
Had been for damp-painted ages... The pedantry of faceless
Decision Makers – unseen Deciders – was just the tip of icy
Burgesses' scorning tongues, their remotest neighbours;
The thoughtless prompt in ventriloquised clauses; the trigger
In a train of contagious thoughts spinning Russian roulettes
In his head, the end of tethers and teleological tropes
Like looped ropes left ominously dangling... So he made his
Decision on behalf of both of them, with punctual timing...
There was also something in the relentless metallic filing-
Cabinet bruise of interminable November skies of low-
Cast murk they scraped under each week on their undernourished
Pilgrimage to Coventry's bombed-out Brutalist miniature
That weighed on them so brutally; they felt themselves burdens,
'Non-contributory' lumpen humps on camel-backs of taxpayers
And habitually *'abused'* auspices of the 'altruistic' state –
To have to justify themselves to a society that wouldn't brook
Their abject and involuntary poverty's insolent stares
Of factual contradiction, instantly shattering of narratives
Fabricated by carrot-and-stick apparatchiks and tsars
At Westminster and Whitehall, as white lies more attractive
To the morals-mortgaged masses than uncomfortable truths
As to their vicarious complicity with claimant-sacrificing;
The Mullins' own community could only accommodate
Their drastically diminished circumstances as the aggregate
Result of their own mistakes and ruinous *'lifestyle choices'*...

4
And there was the Department which required of them
The occulting mystique of a *'something'* in return for precious
Nothing, previous contributions in the only watermarked
Guise governments recognise, not stamps or Co-op coupons
Or invisible achievements that can't be gauged, measured
Or factored-in, for growing in the souls of benefactors
To shadow-volunteering – the non-exchangeable coinage
Of charitable soul-labour *in lieu* of non-entitlements… Curt
Letters elliptically spelt out their fate on sour white vellum,
Onion-sliced from the pelt of the State's hunted Leviathan,
Scourge of its own fiscal Calvinism; but the hardest thing
Of all for the Mullins was to justify themselves to themselves,
Their stubborn cohabiting in 'wageless sin', even though
They had no reason to – *who* was judging? – since they'd tried
Everything to escape their dead-end… And there had
Always been warnings that things couldn't drag on as they did:
Glimmerings in the judgemental dead-eyed semi-grins
Of impersonal jobcentre advisors, derisory coupons dished
Out for battered tins instead of dignity-acknowledging giros,
Or growing *'scrounger'*-mongering of government and red-top,
And public parrot-opinion spitting feathers and coffin-nails
From Social Attitudes Surveys' depleting orange peels
Of compassion fatigues, and bitter curds like lime-scale shavings…
Hounded to honourable oblivions for his soldier's horror
At *'handouts'*, army traumas trampling him in his tracks,
Stacking on his narrow-strapped shoulders, a down-at-heel
Giant's in the drained teabag eyes of his dishcloth wife...
Through those long-rationed days he got through so many
Notches on his noose-loosening belt, tightening it until it split,
The colour rubbing off revealing striations of peeling leather
As on that old, quaintly-battered, red, portcullis-spiked
Suitcase hoisted on Budget days by the cloth-cut Chancellor
Of the Exchequer as a Red Reminder that days of dying
Roses are now over, as nights grow long and days grow leaner…

5

The Mullins were found figuratively snuggled under blankets
In the one heated room of their rundown digs in Bedworth,
Warwickshire, apparently clasped in a pact to make this
Their last winter (and last indigent gesture), obviate veiled
Threats of pincer-movements – her imminent Sectioning,
And a prospect of electrical disconnection to a mockery
Of impotent sockets – and atone to the ratty Nanny State
For its unbefitting benefits, its bitter pills of chewed-up biros,
Haggled giros, foregone wills – not in anger, but forgiveness
For their punishers' loopholes, snares and tripwires, turning
Their other cheeks to pillows from all those obstacles,
Clauses, caveats, sanctions, better move through penury's
Departure lounge than endure being tagged as *'scroungers'*;
Better by far to lay down their lives voluntarily, martyrs
To austerity, fiscal casualties punctual as larks, rustic
Pilots of unacceptable poverties… They took the stigmas
On their palms like stigmata of stinging nettles brushing
Their swaying arms, cagoule-swishing, through swingeing verges
Of rumour-mongering hedgerows catching their sleeves
On snagging bramble-mumbles' *'spongers'*, *'malingerers'*,
Malicious whispers' *'workshy'-ness* – O if all he'd had to cope
With had been work, what luxury of soul, what balm for mind
And body that would have been – but it'd been his lot to be
Condemned to bitter scrimping, and no one to pat him
On the back at the end of each day's punishing shift of trying
To survive, the most soul-destroying of all human occupations
(But the most fundamental), estranging one from everything –
Stung by *entfremdung*; and those shadows that scrounged from
Their wilting spirits in rust-brown autumnal dusks of tight-
Shinned homeward treks, vegetables rumbling in rucksacks,
Ditchwater-thin soups evaporating in tight tureens
Of their gurgling bellies – plunging guts – to the scuff of splitting
Boots and punctured breaths; the buckles on their backpacks
Ringing dimly in the inky village-dark like Lilliputian leper bells
Thinning out into giant tolls of Brobdingnagian nights…

The Bedroom Taxidermy

Unauthorised households no longer have the right to hold
Phantoms and memories hostage in spare rooms, those
Unoccupied pausing spaces, shrines of worship, perfectly-
Kept time-capsules of sons' and daughters' last trails, left
Authentically intact in their absences; or store rooms for
Surplus furniture, blanketed ghoulish shapes – ergonomic ghosts –
Or for keeping equipment to aid disabilities in specially –
And spatially – adapted homes to accommodate them; now
Council households are disallowed phantom *'spare room subsidies'*
For upkeep of such reliquaries, these *'under-occupied'*
Guest rooms for visiting relatives, or domestic carers;
Or occasional stopping-points for offspring returning
To the source of their bloodstreams, to replenish their penuries,
Or, in salmonid pilgrimage, gasp their last in brackish shallows
Of sound surroundings, those hopeless trophy rooms of long-
Pawned childhoods, knowing they'll never be able to make
That leap in shortfall from the precipice of caps, let alone
One day sip the spiced price of ownership, but only be
House-sitters, occupiers of others' sub-let consciousnesses…
Or simply spaces where people can come to stay instead
Of shelling out on B&Bs – in any case, now permanent ports
Of 'temporary' accommodation brimful with refugees from
Same purges of *'spare room subsidies'* – the *'bedroom tax'* by
Bitter sobriquet – or due to rent arrears triggered by caps
To benefits *in lieu* of re-introducing private rent controls –
Those long-abolished elephants on the *'spare'* room: ripe pickings
For tenancy cleansers corpulent with properties, fattening-up
On unfurnished profits, mould-spotted upholsteries; the taint
Of asthma gasped from miasmas of damp pile – Capitalism's
Prime weapon of domestic marsh-gas, secreted to keep its surplus
Population too short of breath to rise up and grasp its auspices,
Churning regimes permanent as trapped phlegm, productive
Coughs of the chronically unproductive, dust-mite fabrics
Of *Shake 'N' Vac* fascism brushed under carpets… This is
The age of regulating indigents but not the triggers of indigence,

While letting 'Buy-to-Let' vet tenants and bet away the shelters
Of fellow citizens – 'Right-to-Buy' for the already propertied,
But *no* 'Right-to-Rent' for the unfunded young relegated
To single rooms or house-sharing (Buy-to-Vet Kibbutz) –
No spatial privileges for moles of huddled hovels, culled
Badgers of bedsits; now, all council homes front-loaded
Onto bowing lobes of drooping-browed windows – no overflow-
Pipes for expelling pressures damned-up to the limits:
The domestic subconscious sub-let to lodgers, tent-veterans
To tenants – *'There's no room left!'* Not even for the converted;
Occupancies cramped up to capacities (yet so many empties!):
No vent for over-crowding: all available space to be topped up
With bodies, the barely living, and the dead in all but arrears,
Un-vaunted auto-icons, bedroom Jeremy Benthams, stuffed toys
And chewed-eared teddy bears with petrified stares, marble eyeballs,
Pin-cushions for consciences, stitched up in partitioned tombs:
Barely-accommodated bundles of bones, limbs, sinews & pent-
Up nerves; beings genetically surcharged to generate rent…

The Significs of Gentrification

Victoria, Lady Welby might have rethought her theory
Of *significs* – the simplification of language to a more
Elliptical set of semiotics, a drainage of vocabularies
To an unambiguous bog of symbols, silage of signs,
Mostly nouns or their lowest common denominators
And the focus on their verbal, volitional and moral purposes –
In order to spurn political manipulation of phrases,
Massaging of meanings and disfiguring figures of speech,
To promote hegemonies of any given period, since
Its' contemporary application by plutocrats and politicians
Is being employed to apply the same principles to
The behavioural persuasiveness of juvenile vocabularies –
'The right thing', 'fairness', 'roll up our sleeves' – O how those
Signs affect us, Monsieur de Saussure, Swiss linguist,
Might have wished, as well as his Significian contemporary,
To finesse his thesis on Pragmatics – the pulling power
Of euphemisms to camouflage the most punishing policies,
So much so, it would seriously unnerve tubercular Eric
Blair's claret-coloured veins to perceive the prolific
Fructification of his prophetic dystopian Newspeak:
'Gentrification' is today's operative term – or signification –
Superimposed upon social purges by chalk-striped pilots
At Westminster to soften the eardrum to the muffled sobs
Of undernourished children torn from their homes,
Communities and schools (classrooms of fainting grounds
For infants in raptures of morning fasts) after their capped
Parents are sifted through shortfalls, forced out from
Tenancies of unregulated rents, or from council houses
For *'under-occupying'* them (*'spare rooms'* they can barely fit
A bed into, cropped by damp thin-walled partitions); some
Are packed off to bed and breakfasts, boarding-houses –
Modern Jude Fawleys and Sue Brideheads – cold weather
Shelters, or the streets, to queue up at pop-up soup kitchens
And flourishing foodbanks – alfresco solutions of filtered
Austerities – *'social cleansing'*, the more critically inclined

Might call it, but in Governmentspeak it is that genteelly
Termed, most acceptable-sounding thing: *'Gentrification'*,
Which sounds so refined and Georgian, greased with
Regency elegance (very Jane Austen!) – the spring-cleaning,
This cruellest April, of buy-to-let speculators' metropolitan
Properties, purged of proles and claimants, state-assisted
Tenants blue-rinsed of rental subsidies and bounced out
On kerbsides, flung onto punishing pavements, forbidden
From burrowing into cobwebbed nooks of abandoned
Buildings, derelict empties, since squatting is now punishable
With prison: Shelter at Her Majesty's Pleasure – monarchy is,
Of course, exempt from this tax on *'under-occupation'*:
The demotic masochism of the patriotic British taxpayer
Knows no bounds: to subsidise thousands of spare rooms,
Boudoirs and chambers honeycombing the Windsors'
Winter palaces, their upkeep and heating (not forgetting
Luxurious kennels for the Corgies and palatial stables
For the horses – the gold-dripping Royals are merely
Reaping dues by heredity, picking choicest berries
Of their branching birthrights, while low-hanging dog-pissed
Drupelets are being robbed by shirking *'arbeitsscheu'*
(*'Workshy'*) bottom-feeders: the poor are always *'scrounging'*,
So hegemonic agitprop and propaganda goes… So right-
Wing Significs pacify the facts by saying to parroting publics,
They are not cleansing or culling or fumigating or pulling rugs
From under underdogs, nor sugaring pills of persecution
With syrupy sprinklings of doughnut churns, but are simply
'Gentrifying' inner-cities, purifying them of misfits and
Refuseniks to fumigating ghettoes, hostels, bedsits – for,
After all, *'Sunlight is the best disinfectant'*, and never more
Cleansing than it is today, sunrays thrown like gold-gilded
Bricks through those windows with *'shut curtains during the day'*
By Savile Row-suited poverty tsars and Hugo Boss-
Skirted austerity tsarinas, who, contrapuntally, refuse
To shine a torch-light into those tinted-windowed boardrooms
Where City *'talent'* alchemises more golden hellos, goodbyes,
And showers of bonuses through the nose, and more besides,
Always knowing the Bullingdon boys are standing up to
Brussels bureaucrats to ring-fence their friends' financial

Incentives, investments and *'business interests'*, and so
Stop them jumping this sinking island for less regulation
Overseas; they must *'incentivise'* the porcine speculators
With more tax-pies, while making work pay dividends
Of divide-and-rule by diminution of stigma, income only
Marginally more generous by comparison to downgrades
Of welfare payments capped to scraps by these hereditarily
Minted battlers of intergenerational entitlements –
They must make it *'easier to employ people'* by snipping
Through the strings of employment rights; scrubbing out
The unions! If Victoria, Lady Welby was alive now, no doubt
She'd carve a caveat into the edifice of her *Significs*, and,
In light of today's rhetorical cull of fiscal cliffs, castigate
Pen-pushing persecutors: ensure *WORDS always pay…*

The Disinfecting Sunlight

*'The shadow is simply the black side of someone's self
personality. What is black is always known only indirectly
through projection upon others.'*
Carl Jung

I   The Girl with the Giro Tattoo

The girl next door but one is suicidal, but has yet
To bring herself to wringing out her veins, nor applying
Swingeing cuts to her wrists, thus severing the link between
Need and entitlement; a little letting might settle the bet,
Hack back the nettles of tan paper tensions, or swigs
Of sunlight-disinfectant; in the meantime, she's beholden
To arbiters of taboo dependencies; but she does her bit
For the sacrifices of austerity: self-harms daily by
Branding her arms with a molten-hot mould embossed
With the stigmatising insignia of the claimant –
The branded puss-filled bubo of the jobless, raised weal
Of the giro tattoo… Each such undecided Senecan
Disciple needs a dialectical drip-feed to cut across
The moral question of their psychical short-cut; to cut
To the chase, and cut across the other side of the hedge
Like the quick brown fox *vulpes purpureus alacercris*…

Time to spring into escape, dart off before the dawn raids
Of brown envelopes pounce through the letter-box like barking
Foxhounds with the scent of hircine claimants in their soggy
Nostrils, osmagogue of *'scrounger'*, spice of scapegoat –
Time for the hunt of urban foxes, the encroaching apocalypse
Of black spots, triangulations of black, bruise-black,
Night of the eye-patch of tick-boxed *'useless eaters'*,
Hungry unbelievers thronging for soup-kitchen ablutions,
Food bank baptisms, hopeless eyes like surrendered soup coupons
For thin broths spiced with carroty soupçons, desperate
Apostles of alfresco socialism outsourced by
Whitehall Pilates as capitalism is re-centralised, rationalised,
Concentrated in pincers of onion-slicing exchequers…

II Scroungerology

The suicidal girl finds her benefits stripped, her children capped,
Her roof time-limited, as the street of shut curtains is
Gentrified of short-falling rents, bleached of penniless tenants,
Crumbling battlements beset by serried lettings signs
Hauled up to hector: *TO LET* …but *NOT* to *YOU*… or *YOU* –
Especially if on benefits, the big taboo, last of the acceptable
British anti-shibboleths sponsored by Pontius Pilate & Sons
Letting Agents (who won't let any claimants in) and Buy-To-
Vet private landlords invoking acquisitive vows of proscriptive
Sieving to the grasping trinity of unregulated demiurges:
Property, Profit, Portfolio… Each residential street, a stucco-
Golgotha where the Og, Gog, Magog, osmagogue, Cro-Magnon,
Scrounger-Ogre and Giro-Troll of modern red-top mythopoeia,
Our common mythology, home grown symbology, Scroungerology,
Are figuratively crucified every day under the newly blessed
Apocryphal Eleventh Commandment: *'Thou Shalt Not Accept DSS'*…

'No DSS. No smokers. No pets. No children. No students. No dossers.
No scroungers. No Chavs. No lascars. No lazars. No social lepers. No
ASBOs. No NEETS. No WRAGS. No Roma. No single mothers.
No dependents. No pets on benefits. No poets. No smoking tortoises.
No dogs on giros. No dipsomaniacal goldfish. No parrot squatters.
No workshy cats. No self-harmers. No wrist-slitters. No curtain-shutters.
No daylight-dodgers…
                   For sunlight is the best disinfectant…'

The workless classes are floated on the markets to go
To the lowest bidders, workfare for a lip-served wage,
Peanuts compared to what it will be when the Eton Blues
Repatriate the Working Time Directive and pass off
Paltry scraps for apprenticeships as part-payment
Of a phantom minimum wage, tighten up the torque
Of the workhouse yoke round turkey necks of graduates
And claimants; no more entitlements or rights, now poverty
Itself is a privilege – and has, in any case, been swiftly
Redefined (by those who have never suffered it) to something
More than material deprivation (which it is: it also strips

The spirit – and, sometimes, paradoxically, the appetite),
Something, conceivably, if one might indulge a germ
Of sociological gerrymandering, that actually has nothing
To do with income: after all, there's more to life than money,
Except for the rich who are particularly susceptible
To the pinch: *They* must be incentivised with tax cuts
And loopholes (*Render unto Cayman*, and all that), top ups
And bonuses at the expense of taxpayers, but the poor
Can only be motivated by threats to strip their benefits
This is termed *'nudging'*; while *'hardworking taxpayers'*
Are incentivised via the recidivist gutter press
To vent their spleen in vilifying welfare claimants, even
Vilifying themselves, since most of the *'bloated'* welfare budget's
Spent on those *in work*, and will be even more so since
The Tories are tempting the middle classes with carrots
Of childcare vouchers most of them don't need, bonuses
For the bourgeois, pips for the *'squeezed middle'*, while those
Who do need state assistance are left with even less
At the bottom of the pit – this is the Gentrification
Of the Welfare State (Attlee and Bevan must be spitting
In their graves!): to provide a safety net purely for those
Who have enough spare to pay into it, while sifting out
The neediest; and how has this been justified? Through
Scapegoat legerdemain, shadow-projecting sleight-of-hand:
Red-top and parliamentary implicature that passes for
Dialectic – Hegelian engineering: thesis, antithesis and synthesis,
Each simply states *'unemployed'/ 'poor'* = *'sponger', 'scrounger',*
'Shirker', 'skiver' (as opposed to *'striver'* – *O 'survival*
Of the fittest'! – such simplistic binary disfigurement
Of argument, the truth sacrificed for the sake of a half-rhyme) –
O how many times is brittle Britishness to latch onto
The red-top pitch of punishing the unemployed for
Their unemployment, the scourge of 'Scroungerphobia'
In the Seventies and Eighties grows into a more aggressive
'Scroungerology' in the Noughties through Noughteens –
We've been here before: Pete Golding's *Images of Welfare*,
Never more relevant a text, and Jim Allen and Roland Joffe's
The Spongers should be repeated on TV to spike the skewered
Welfare anti-debate of today, recrudescent from yesterday –

The juxtaposition of its emotive title superimposed
On blow-ups of the Queen and Duke of Edinburgh amidst
Bunting of the Silver Jubilee, still an apposite polemical
Quip in contemporary society; but anything for the Brits
Than the tougher task of questioning the ethical fabric
Of a monarchy they're apparently happy to support
As taxpayers at the expense of supporting the poorest,
In spite of its superabundant ability to support itself
Through vast capital of palatial properties and crown lands;
And anything to squaring up to pinstriped City culprits,
Toking bonuses at their expense, *'forestalling'* till tax breaks
Come in, hoarding profits spilling through butter-fingered
Light-touch Tory non-dom monitoring; siphoning it off
To offshore havens, 'patriotic' hypocrites who'd jump ships
To Switzerland at the merest hint of regulation, abandon
Their nation at a time of national need, as they already do
While still domiciled here; refusing to lend, nor even pretend
They're anything other than the venal swine most suspect
They are – but the fiscal cliffs are summoning these Gaderene
To trip off the edge in their glad rags and *'respectable greed'*…

III The Doughnut Churn

Workers denied overtime for surpluses of unemployed
Post-graduates crimped into exploitative placements
Of shelf-stacking slave labour to buoy corporate returns
For Asda, Tesco – *'Every Little Bit Helps'*; *'Everything Must Go';*
Everything Must Churn; Let it all churn! Everything, every piece
Of the apparatus, each bit of furniture, even the old rickety
Attleean portmanteau, the Bakelite Bevanite medicine cabinet –
All out the door, and with barely a mandate, going for a song,
Along with the poor, out into the *'doughnut ghettoes'* they go,
Or onto the streets, or the draughty floors of Samaritans'
Emporiums for *'sofa-surfing'*, rockpools of bought time
As rents go through the roofs, and the only way out
Is the only way in for this lobbyists' labyrinth: one in,
One out, through the *'poor doors'*, on the rota, *'BACK into
Work'* (BARK: *WORK!*), whether poorly paid, voluntary,
Or paid in poverty, the Tories' way of 'making work pay' –
Freeze wages, herd indigents through the cast-iron gates
To freedom: freedom is serfdom:
For sunlight is the best detergent…

Now is the time of the urban churn, the herding
Of the narrowest shoulders out from narrow houses and
Carpet-capped communities, out, out into the big sobriety,
To sink or swim, or surf a sea of sofas, or play
At origami with cardboard in the chilly porchways –
Churn, churn, let it all churn as undesirables
Are edged out into *'doughnut-ghettoes'*, a doughnut churn
Of un-sugared sourdough doles to lodge in the oesophagus
Of *'scroungers'*, a cherry pick of red tops for the proles,
Bespoke coffees, rapturous brown soups sipped by
An expert *'precariat'* happy that they're permitted to smoke
Outside public cafes, alternately tanning or rinsing themselves
On pavement-patios… Let it all churn so much so
That people won't notice, only the politicians and speculator
Parasites of the private rental sector, the Buy-To-Bet
Brobdignangians with their candy-topped portfolios set
To squash the scurrying Lilliputian occupants…

And all the while the suicidal girl feels her rumbling guts
Churning, especially in the mornings, churning with almost
Unendurable dread of terrible thoughts being substantiated –
And so on the rumble and rumpus unfed but for prefab
Endorphins of drip-fed caffeine in the synthetic glare
Of cotton-stopped bottles like sweet jars by her bed…

IV Hyperkulturemia

The girl next door but one, she had to get away from
The uncompromising richness of the contemporary,
She thirsted for austerity, craved authenticity,
The hand-to-mouth, to not have enough to put on her plate –
If one has their full portion how do they appreciate…?
Most of all she needed escape from other people,
Unemployment was the passport out from social phobia,
Pressures of impersonal employment, its suppression
Of the personality, to pureness of reclusion in penury,
A prescription for privation, for very private poverty,
Through non-passport benefits, she had to get away,
Not physically, but hypothetically, what politicians
Would term *'morally'*, shut herself away with the curtains
Drawn conscientiously throughout the day, her
Invisibility a psychical magnet behind the crushed chintz,
Thoughts frigid, disfigured, fragile, taut as asthmatic lungs –
To draw the espionage of neighbours, the stigmatising
Scorn of dawn workers passing her curtain-drawn window,
So pleased with themselves for having jobs they hate,
And that, somehow, they'd be paid much better if it wasn't
For the blasted Welfare State, so soured with resentments
At the taxes the Government keeps telling them are
Effectively stolen from them by benefit recipients
In an automatic manner tantamount to *'mugging'* …the sun,
The city's lurid colours, the tortuous miniatures of every street
And painted face became too much for her to take in anymore –
She must, ultimately, cure her hyperkulturemia…

And in so many ways the Government had done this for her:
Now she was clinging by her anchoritic nails
Onto the brickwork up until the point the caps kicked in
And a tax put on her spare broom cupboard pushed up
Her rent towards arrears and eviction procedures –
While thumbscrewers at jobcentreplus applied due protocols
And pressures to *'disrupt and upset'* her… And, inescapably,
All this upset her appetite, a pity, but perhaps of more
Than metaphorical purposes, since she was by her incapacity
A self-perceived *'useless eater'*, perennially torn between
'Heating or eating', and in her lightheaded anxiety –
Her effortless fasting – she knew at gut-level that to eat
Was to keep oneself on earth, thus prolonging the agony
Of anticipated premature departure, protracting
The chronic, putting off the unaccomplished fact…

But the worst affliction of all whelmed up from within her,
The constant churn in the pit of her stomach,
Churn of a soul-hunger unable to be alleviated
By anything readily edible, not by any known comestible,
Only by the unpurchaseable nourishment of the spiritual,
Purgation through the thurible of her bile-choked throat
As it spilt back out the compounds pestled into little
White pills which she swallowed by the score straight
From the cotton-wool-stopped cloudy gallipots,
Surprising herself most of all, for she thought she hadn't
The bottle to go through with it – but it was in actual fact
The churn that decided it, alleviated temporarily after
The acid reflux and regurgitation, as the underlying dry thirst,
After the purge, and that unmistakeable backwash
Of phantom carrots on the tongue's dehydrated tureen –
Now all she can taste is carrot, and a hint of arrowroot seasoning –
And don't they say carrots help us see in the dark…?

…the dark, the dark, the Kierkegaardian dark,
O Kierkegaard, where art thou in our hour of need
When the dredge of Dread grinds and churns its plough-blades
Through the black peat of Jutland angst?
Where's the Dane when one needs him?
There's only in his place the Other One,
The blond suicidal Prince contemplating impossible nothing
Glowing like a blackening sun…

The girl with the giro tattoo has been bathing her mind
In too much bleak Nordic Noir and Ingmar Bergman gloom,
Time to rip open shut curtains, let light pour in the room –
Too late the light now that she's poured liquid light
Down into her throat's dimming tomb… now her soul
Outgrows its organic projection, pitches into wholesome shadow
That blots and slowly spreads upon her seeping pillow…

…It has to get light before it gets dark, and O
It can't get dark too soon… Only in the dark, the pitch
Dark, the pitch black, can shadows be subsumed,
Obscured, unobserved…

For disinfectant is the best sunlight…

Going Dutch

The head of the table tells us we've *'maxed out our credit card'*,
That *'there isn't any money left'* in the collective kitty, so, to cut
A long story short, from henceforth it's every household for
Itself, we can no longer accommodate a national slate, nor
A tab to be picked up by the taxpayer, so it's pretty much
Curtains for the welfare state (at least in terms of assisting
The neediest: all that's left is to gentrify what remains of it
To keep a safety net for those who can afford to pay into it) –
Our flirtation with *'fairness'* has ended in failure, near-bankruptcy,
'Benefits dependency', and has long reached the point of no returns
For levied investors in government evergetism – those grumpy
Number scribblers, most unlikely contributors to the common good –
Or rood, resistant auto-altruists of cropped acquisitiveness;
In spite of ancient precedent, the only thing certain in Tory Britain
Is death, while it avoids its taxes – no more *'mugging the taxpayer'*
By the unemployed, under-employed and crime syndicates
Of under-classes (banditti of *'useless eaters'*), for now the meal's long
Been digested, that old soul food, and the bill's arrived,
And is being scrutinised item by item through pairs of designer
Oblong lenses and costs meted out equidistantly each according
To their feeds, in spite of direr needs, the splitting of the bill is
In process (the splitting of atomism), meticulous as dissection
Or autopsy, and will set the future precedent henceforth,
So each pays according to their means (or mains), and the less
Their means then the less they'll eat – or heat, as the case may be;
For the first time in such a fundamental sense since the difficult
Birth of the long-depleted Attlee Settlement, England's *'Going
Dutch'* at the table of national repast, of finger-dipping
Feudal fondue, after all they've been doing this in Holland all along,
And it's catching on the Continent, a new dining etiquette
In twelve-starred restaurants everywhere, replete with a new range
Of ever-diminishing menus, and in this sense the English are
Getting back in touch with their ancestors, at least, those
Descendants of Norman Barons, or genetic Huguenots
With Protestant tailor progenitors (a la all 'English' thoroughbred

Nigel Farages for instance, and spouted flat rates appropriated
From flatlands) – tan envelopes are being passed round the table,
Some fat with notes, others slimmer, empty except for thinly-
Veiled threats and notices of withdrawal of benefits as hinted
Slyly through Dutch windows on their fronts; England might
Only be open for business and xenophobia, and primed for *coitus
Interruptus* of the European experiment, but when it comes to
Domestic economics and staunching further spillages
Of redistribution (or dampening them through fiscal Dutch caps),
It's macro-economically cosmopolitan, draws inspiration
From the country of tulips, cycling, windmills, Edam, Rembrandt,
Vincent van Gogh and clogs, comfortably – for some – below
Sea-level, as laterally trickling Amsterdam, and well below
The spirit-level, more split-level – England's *'Going Dutch' – Again!*
So, indigent diners, be sure to order the cheaper suppers,
Spare the specials for your pecuniary superiors, stick to
Affordable poor-door dishes for your improvised mains, and
No sneaky green-eyed peaking from behind your menus' blinders…

Auld Reekie's Black Spot

i.m. Paul Reekie, 1962-2010

The suicide notes – there were two – were formal curios:
One said, in stuttering Courier New: *'We write to inform you*
That you have been found fit for work, so will no longer be
In receipt of incapacity benefit as of...' the numbers shook
His drowsy head awake, the dates might well have been
Engraved on his own headstone; the other note, again,
In Courier New, or possibly Arial, he couldn't be sure –
And felt too broken to bother checking on his dying
Computer (and certainly no point consulting his obsolete
Cobwebbed typewriter crouched like a mummified
Arachnid husk in the corner of the room) – it said
The same as the first letter, only this time in relation
To his Local Housing Allowance, partly as a knock-on
Effect of passport and non-passport domino shibboleths…

So that was pretty much it. He dusted himself off for last
Orders at *The Artisan*, a pint or two of Dutch, a tipping
Yellow froth like pissed-on snow, and slowly-emptying
Saloon bar for his mundane, damp-elbow-on-soggy-beer-towel
Gethsemane… Days on – this was some time in June,
Quite when, we can't be sure – he bowed out in a boozy slumber,
The two typed letters from the DWP (Department for
Waifs & Poets…?), two black spots for his Black Dog
(But bounties for Atos for having wrung him out to dry
From the WRAG, keelhauled his soul) left by his bedside,
Playwright pirate R.I.P.; no more Furies of buff envelopes
To terrorise his impecunious obscurity, no, no
More of those suicide seeds pouched in tan or ecru
To hound his hardy reputation, his almost-forgotten
Glaswegian *'genius'*, lost now to underground edible
Printing inks, damp-blue depressions, used-up nibs…

A fugitive campaign's Black Triangle was raised from
The bruising shadow of his memory, a pitch-black prism
In his name now blotting, blotting, clotting on the Xeroxed
Grain of corpse-white bone-bleached Departmental paper…

Every punishing day the Department for War on the Poor –
Circuitously, through the bones of Atos bounties –
Pays tribute to his forty-eight years by trampling
The beneficent path of Nineteen Forty-Eight, in capping
And cutting, guillotining the post-War consensus, dragging
Back the Welfare State to before the Attlee Settlement,
Before it even settled, reducing numberless
Others through remorseless rounds of brown Robins
To random numbers, as it reduced Paul Reekie to
ONE NINE SIX TWO SLASH TWO ZERO ONE ZERO

Clapson's Cap

i.m. David Clapson (1952-2013)

> 'Her son, compelled, the country's foes had fought,
> Had bled in battle; and the stern control
> Which ruled his sinews and coerced his soul
> Utterly poisoned life's unmingled bowl,
> And unsubduable evils on him brought.'
> Shelley, 'A Tale of Society as It Is: From Facts, 1811'

'Sorry for your loss but no errors were made'
Only those within the margins of human decency –
Well outside the remit of the Dee Double-u Pee,
Only Work Programmes and the worst laid schemes;
No searching of consciences, only search engines on bogus
Job sites of phantom vacancies, and plenty of penalties,
Plethora of sanctions, interrogations, black spots –
And *threats* of all these; dockets for food banks,
Sticks without carrots, punishments, punishments,
Roll up, roll up for punishments – all at the expense
Of soul-and-body nourishments: treat the poor and
Unemployed as if they were pirates ransacking
The public purse (supplied by *'hardworking taxpayers'*),
Daylight-dodgers rolling giros, Black Dog *'Scroungers'*;
Make the unemployed walk the plank, *Nudge 'em, nudge 'em,
Keelhaul 'em*; and as for those malingerers, keep on
Their case, *badger them* – Sheriff stars for badges, *Targets,
Targets*, throw Atos darts at 'em, *'disrupt and upset'* them;
Cap their benefits, splice the mainbrace, clap them in
Irons of no income, as they did with Clapson:
Penalised for missing a jobcentre appointment, stripped
Of his £71.70 weekly allowance, died penniless
And half-starved at 59, collapsed from ketoacidosis
Because he couldn't chill his life-sustaining insulin
In the fridge for the electricity had been cut off
As a result of losing his benefits, all for missing
One single appointment on the Work Programme…

(Mark Wood, a painter, poet and music composer,
Went the same way after Atos declared him *'fit for
Work'* and stopped his benefits, a verdict he sleepily
Accepted – since he always *worked* at his poetic
Occupations, soul's vocations – and one which sapped
His appetite; fitting, since he could no longer afford
To feed himself: when he finally passed out, then passed
Away, aged 44, six stone was all he weighed…)

Clapson, a diabetic ex-soldier, had served in Northern
Ireland at the height of the Troubles, but whom no tours
Of duty on fractious bullet-cracking Belfast streets
Could prepare for the front line of domestic cuts
Under Iain Duncan Smith's punishing welfare regime;
So much for poppies and patriotism, for saying *'We
Will remember them'*, when this vindictive government
Is so quick to forget them; countless souls as Clapson:
No *'scrounger'*, he'd worked and paid his taxes for 29
Years – done Cameron's *'right thing'* – and looked after
His sick mother, thus saving thousands for *'the taxpayer'*,
Then, on her entering a care home, he lost his carer
Status and was put on precarious benefits while
He looked for jobs, and took up unpaid work placements…
Clapson's body was discovered in a sea of CVs and
Job applications, just £3.44 to his name, a tin of soup,
Half a dozen tea bags and an out-of-date can of sardines,
All that was left in his larder – during the post-mortem
The coroner noted no food in his stomach, no food in…
Nothing… *'Something for nothing', something for no tins*,
But nothing in compensation for his petitioning sister,
No formal acknowledgement of 'administrative manslaughter',
Simply a paltry 'apology' as if issued from impartial
Mourners implicitly divorcing themselves from any
Culpability: *'Please Omit Flowers', Please Omit Powers…*

'Sorry for your loss but no errors were made'
The loss is to all of us, to our collective soul,
Our sense of *'good old English decency'* – what values
Have they who throw away the lives of the victims
Of impoverishment and incapacity
For the sake of saving corpses' pennies for the taxpayers?
We say not simply we will remember Clapson
And the tens of thousands of fiscal sacrifices
At the Satanic altar of Austerity – but we say,
All of us, afflicted by the aristocratic Chancellor
And Iain Duncan Smith's administrative massacre
Of the claimants, brandishing our black triangles,
Giro stigmas, stars of David, with rustling wings
Of ominous brown paper envelopes, in the name
Of the Spartacus Report: *We* are Clapson, *We* are
Clapson, *We* are Clapson, *We* are Clapson, *We* are…

'Sorry for your loss but no errors were made'

Sorry for the errors but no loss was made

Tan Raptures

'Consider the ravens: for they neither sow nor reap; which neither have storehouse nor barn; and God feedeth them: how much more are ye better than the fowls?'
Luke 12:24

'Like the said presaging Raven, that Tolls the sick man's passport in her holy beak'
Christopher Marlow, *The Jew of Malta*

'That ill angel the Rauen... a Continuall messenger... of dole and misfortune'
Thomas Nashe, *Terrors Night*

'Like to the fatall ominous Rauen which tolls, The sick mans dirge within his hollow beake'
Edward Guilpin, *Skialethia*

'One cannot help but wonder at this constantly recurring phrase 'getting something for nothing', as if it were the peculiar and perverse ambition of disturbers of society. Except for our animal outfit, practically all we have is handed to us gratis. Can the most complacent reactionary flatter himself that he invented the art of writing or the printing press, or discovered his religious, economic, and moral convictions, or any of the devices which supply him with meat and raiment or any of the sources of such pleasure as he may derive from literature or the fine arts? In short, civilization is little else than getting something for nothing.'
James Harvey Robinson (1863-1936)

First Rapture: Disruptive Patterns

That August, attitudes hardened like tarred arteries,
Latched on to tattered narratives tagged with gutter-grease
Auguring an autumn of hostile posted territories:
The most brutal month was September, as austerity
Throttled the wilting trees, shaking off their brittle leaves
Like burdens that heaped the pavements, as rustlings
Of tan paper envelopes flapped down like mass-arrivals
Of ravens, tan ravens, piling up on lumpen doormats
In paper dispensations; crackling papyri
In variegated shades of greys, browns, umbers and buffs
Like patches on disruptive pattern camouflage fatigues
Swishing through Wootton Bassett's bunting-strung streets:
Processions of rosehip berets trooping after coffins
Of fallen comrades – now empty helmets left behind
Like half-finished coffees, discarded flat whites – spared
The bitter taste of manila damnations that hatched in wait
To ambush traumatised veterans and amputees
Deracinated into civvies, sieved through Cinderella
Psychiatric services (in cinders after scorched earth blitzing
By private carpetbaggers) into combat zones of poverties,
Unemployment and stripes-stripping Atos court-marshals
To shouts of hectoring drill-sergeant administrators
Baying for bounties on backs of 'our boys' 'brownouts;
Caramels salted with spite, hard-boiled *Werther's Originals*;
Lozenges of government's malignant origami
So easily transfigured into three-dimensional guns
Of anguish with primed anxiety-triggers, disclosing
Semantic cyanide capsules and other last ditch provisions
Of proscriptive conditions in case the claimant's captured
And interrogated on tape-recorders, more rigid
Regimental drills of mind than these demobbed press-ganged
Gagging rankers marched to in the services, such loaded
Ammunition in apparently innocuous tropes
As to *'offering further support'* through *'work-focused interviews'*
For the chronically unfocused, bespoke encryptions
To push buttons with blunt instruments, varied alerts,
Amber for ambiguous agonising, *'spinning plates'*

Of red for *'missed targets'*, green for *'hits'* of camouflaged
'Off flows' (every day's 'games day' for jobcentreplus managers,
Sport for the DWP!) – agued insurgents of a mythical
'Something for nothing' culture, abruptly *'taken out of the game'* –
Disruptive patterns of Afghanistan-duty fatigues replaced
By *'disrupt and upset'* protocols of Customer Compliance
Compassion fatigues, and paper trails of memes, mines,
Tripwires and loopholes for post-traumatic sappers
And veterans to navigate on home turf: a fight for survival
In the nation they served to protect from phantom Islamists,
Now wondering if their sacrifices were worth it, under this
Salami-slicing Damocles of departmental Damascening:
A bumpy demobbing from spit-and-polished boots to burnt
Rubber trainers of giro-recruits targeted by red-top
Snipers' anti-*'scrounger'* Agincourt salutes; tours
Of itinerant duties, alfresco ceremonies of soup kitchens,
Trooping the dolour of food banks, or pitching down on
Pavements with upturned berets at their feet catching coins
On cardboard prayer mats defacing scuffed Mecca;
Or snatched up as conscripts for street-vendors of the *Big*
'Society' Issue touting bluntly worded Tory Torah:
'A hand up, not a hand out' – hope-pitched Lottos;
Napoleon Hill's chill-pills to spill like poppy-seeds into furrows
Of Gabriel Tarde's *'grooves of borrowed thought'* – *'TTFN, LIFO'*…

Second Rapture: *Compassion Fatigues*

Otherwise, outside the Ruritanian micro-climate
Of *'Royal'* Wootton Bassett – uchronian Duchy of Grand
La-La-Land, all lions and unicorns, sliced white and brown bread –
Buff uniforms were the ran-tan tunics of paper armies,
Rustling jackets of camel, taupe, ecru, chamoisee and fallow
Of compassion fatigues, khakis and tans; frantic tans
That snatched away precarious securities; lightning tans
That struck twice in the same place, threatening thunder
Of rumbling repercussions; tarnishing tans that assigned
New stars of stigma castigating claimants as guilty by nature
Of circumstances until proven not to be *'scroungers', 'spongers',
'Parasites', 'malingerers'*, layabouts and reprobates;
Sanctioning tans that carried speedy verdicts from so-called
'Decision Makers', deskbound Valkyries swayed by swerving
Ravens of daylight savers reporting suspicions of fraudulent
Neighbours *'on the fiddle'*, snitching on suspected *'benefit cheats'*
Caught working *'cash-in-hand'* while in receipt of state
'Handouts', 'mugging the taxpayer', moonlighting on the side
To top up inadequate doles deemed, nonetheless, *'too generous'* –
Woe betide those not declaring crumbs while claiming scraps!
Ontic tans that latched onto thanatotic instincts,
Catching on nervous fabrics like tan tarantulas or camel
Spiders of constant fateful anticipations; shattering tans
Which were so many flapped punishments, signed and sealed
Arrest warrants in all but name, euphemised as *'Customer
Compliance Procedures'*, gummed gendarmes, licked lictors
Invested with powers to reprimand, prosecute, sentence,
Punish and damn – tan paper which, once opened, could snap
Like a clam, taking off singed fingers; Faustian tans
That demanded eternal fealty, ate away the soul with threat
Of mortal penalty – the threat itself, punishment aplenty;
Tantalus tans that taunted with inadequate *'awards'* lifting
Branches of bare minimums just out of reach, keeping streams
Of income just below chins of subsistence; arbitrary
Tans that could, depending on caprice, metamorphose
Into passports that tipped recipients over threshold frontiers

Into less spiteful territories for supplemental titbits,
Or sphincter-shrink into unspoken *'couple penalties'*;
(Powers that be don't want the unemployed to reproduce);
Sisyphan tans that heaped more problems and conditions
Than assistance on one's plate: so-called *'overpayments'*
Clawed back with small warning, so after tortuous protocols
And belated payments in, soon payments went back out,
Each giro a giant boulder pushed up to the top of the pile
Only to roll down again (on the dole the only way's downhill)…
Puritan tans that instructed austere penances of fasting
And self-flagellating regimens of mind; Catholic tans
That transubstantiated bread back into paper, assigning
Guilt to rack the rag and *'Wrag'*, offering forgiveness
Only for those who paid indulgences in indigence,
But none for those who confessed to micro-offences
While tape-recorded; black and tans that sprang dawn raids
On unsuspecting claimants, to terrorise and administratively
Traumatise them; Malthusian tans that called time on tenancies
With slashing cuts and caps to phantom *'spare room subsidies'*
(The very real *'bedroom tax'*), or served as recyclable Dutch caps:
No entitlements for any third child born to unemployed
Parents (Iain Duncan Smith's guillotining Herod Clause);
Anxious tans that sent recipients into instant flaps,
Palpitations, panic attacks, hearts pounding, pulses thumping
Into fight-or-flight responses, slashed through shredded nerves
Like knives through margarine, or deadened them altogether
Into Dido ideations, making many tan martyrs
Of auto-raptures, spontaneous raptures of unreported
Populations self-topped on autopilots for want of top ups
To pots of copper pennies left unspent, stripped of paltriest
Spending power, stripped of hope, unable to cope, at the end
Of the rope, pipped at the post like so many metaphorical
Falcon Scotts torn between *'heating or eating'* in the igloo-
Glooms of kitchen-sink Antarctics, haunted by their own
Future frostbitten ghosts, pale shadows who took themselves
Up in tan raptures after their benefits were stopped by
Colophons of apocryphal reports from Atos, Maximus
And Capita declaring them *'fit for work'*, their obscured cases

Documented on un-consecrated grounds at *Calum's List*
And the Black Triangle Campaign domain to the chagrin
Of the DWP that sought to suppress them, an aggregate
Never highlighted in the mainstream media (*we pray for those
Who took up tan raptures for the sakes of cash-strapped taxpayers…*)

Third Rapture: *Eudemonia Ends in Damascene Moment*

Tan panic was rife after that first austere summer; swiftly
Set in with autumn's dismantlement set forth in that thorny
Stone-cast statement enunciated on the chill wind
Of the icy Chancellor's thin, vindictive, reedy voice,
Periodically broken by the harshness of its own draconian
Doctrine, sporadic sips of water used to lubricate his
Rasping hoarseness, help his throat swallow the sharp sparks
Of flinty options, stones thrown violently – his sort
'Love the sound of broken glass' – as fiscal missiles
At the voiceless and most vulnerable from the merciless
Rostrum of the dispatch-box; the mythology of *'something
For nothing'* augmented by old Etonians on the slippery
Perspiring *'playing fields'* of green benches, and administered
In a scattering of tan ravens on pauperised recipients,
Ripe pickings for vultures of private sector scavengers,
Prey to corporate raptors, incapacity asset-strippers,
Outsourced Furies and sub-contracted Harpies – Capita,
Serpica, Carilion, G4S, A4e; now social security
Was grist for rictus and craw – a harvest of autumn tans
Flapped down on doormats of austerity's first casualties –
The easily picked-off poor, victims of cash shavings,
Carrion for *'fiscal consolidation'*... or, beneficiaries
Of Salvation through ever-severer poverties in the feverous
Rapture of a Sandhurst-educated ex-Scots Guards Officer-
Cum-monastic fantasist turned pinstriped Saul of Tarsus
Thunderstruck in a lachrymose Damascus moment
In Easterhouse when a fork of lightning hit the thick skull
Of his domed head with a miraculous solution to the chronic
Quandary of under-consumption in the midst of overt
Reproduction: this shaven-scalped savant with Shavian veins,
This unlikely Miracle Man, arrived at a dialectical
Cul-de-sac which his distant uncle several times reproved,
Old badger-bearded George Bernard Shaw, would have balked at
As a Malthusian short straw for the poor: end the days
Of eudemonia, lift the long-term unemployed up out
Of the belching pits of penury by the boot-straps of their paltry alms,
And emancipate them onto another plane of consciousness,

A new form of human flourishing *sans* nourishing,
Where money perished like withering flowers starved of daylight –
'They are NOT suffering' stressed IDS of those he'd made destitute,
The only true *'suffering'* is to be *'left on the scrapheap'*
Of long-term unemployment (especially if prey to private
Sector work capability assessors appointed by his department),
That is *'moral'* *'suffering'*, far more injurious to the soul
Than mere empty bellies, red reminders and repossessions;
And in this penniless abyss he'd swing his wrecking ballpoint pen
Across cream paper under swingeing green portcullis, then,
With regimental precision, adjust his cufflinks before dealing
His recumbentibus: mass eviction of the poorest and lamest
Towards mandatory transmigration of doles, compulsory
Diaspora of the unemployed – as the tan raven flies…

Fourth Rapture: *Something for Nothing*

Damascus Smith's accidental dialectic, had he the cut
To articulate it, is that old puritanical calling-card,
That Calvinistic chestnut, the double-sided coin
Of psychological egoism, mint of the following argument:
That altruism is its own reward, geared more towards
The moral gratification of the giver through the granting
Of alms to the open-palmed poor, benefits for the *'feckless'*,
The *'something for nothing'* rigmarole, thus a reward
Which is in itself a *'benefit'* in a piece of pity circuitously
Bequeathed via the receiver back to the giver – though hardly
What Auguste Comte meant by it – thus, as well as being
An act of moral self-indulgence for the giver, serves
To morally rob the recipient of their right to dignified
Indigence by short-changing their spiritual appetites
With mere material bribes which might keep body, but not
Soul, together, and be detrimental to their already
Fraying moral fibres (not to mention mortal souls) –
'There's more to poverty than simply lack of money!' so minted
Tories tell us: that might be so, but surely the solution
Isn't to dole out *even less? 'Man cannot live by bread alone'* –
No, but he still needs *some* bread, else he cannot live *at all*…
According to Damascus Smith's Humpty-Dumpty argument,
It's far better, nobler and moral to deny the needy what
They need, and so save their souls even if not their bodies
(Which is a better long-term investment promising greater
Returns, and nudging rapider rehabilitations); how
Ingenious, this flipping of the moral coin, what a truly
Altruistic Scripture scrolls out from Caxton House –
Comte would be proud? – in Courier New correspondences
Enclosed in tan paper raptures, so profound, paradoxical,
Sublime, ahead of its time – Lo! Behold! We live in the midst
Of prophet-politicians, forget your chiliasm, this is
As chilling as it gets: do we not now walk hand-in-hand
With our God, our wounding Woden, God of the Back-to-Work
Wicca, bow down to the cult of the Work God (for the old God,
The woolly-headed one with cloudy beard and bottle-top
Glasses, that old gradualist God of bygone Fabian days,

Is now well and truly dead, deaded, deadest, while
The pinstriped mint-ruminating demiurge of the DWP
Thinks he knows best, better, bested, and is having all
The Lazarus skivers raised from the dead, has sub-contracted
Atos to kick away their crutches while they're tipped out
Of their wheelchairs into Capita's soapy spas for *'spongers'*
(Lourdes lidos buried deep in Brutalist office blocks)? Cleansed
Through Maximus's miracle cures of Work Capability
Assessments that make the unfit *'fit for work'* – for today's
Sick chits are now transformative *'fit notes'*! And Pontius Pilate
GPs compromise their Hippocratic Oaths, and ten-a-penny
Occupational Therapists tie up their prescriptive consciences
And let descriptors do the dirty for them – the incapacitated
Are stressed, tested, sentenced: sentenced to non-existent *'work'* –
Work, our Tetragrammaton; so much for Gospel aphorisms:
Now not even Primrose progressives consider the ravens
Who've ever enjoyed Nature's unconditional basic income…

Fifth Rapture: *Note on Alms*

O how wrong we were about those Tory howlers, those
Howling wolves waving fang-white papers when the ice-
Cut Chancellor first brandished his slicing incisors
And swooped in like a cape-winged vampire bat to sink
Them deep into the Attleean neck, for this was not,
As we had thought, to drain the blood of the poorest
And palest, but was oppositely an act of emergency
Moral transfusion: the emptier the belly, the fuller the spirit!
How wrong we were to rush to judgement, how blind for
The glare of the howling Tory Torch, the howl of the Tory Torah!
To think we used such callow phrases as 'fiscal holocaust'
And *'social cleansing'* when, now, six years on and – at the last
Recorded count – 91,740 departed souls later,
(All gifted the privilege to transcend through tan raptures,
Lifted up by winged angels granting hand ups, to be *'born
Again'* and sign on in the great jobcentreplus-in-the-sky),
Suspected abuses of disability rights to be investigated by
The U.N., a special rapporteur to inspect tan raptures,
But precious little fanfare of such scandal from the press –
Now we can see more clearly how those howls were not the howls
Of cupidity and callousness on behalf of taxpayers
Recouping compulsorily snapped-up scraps of pay,
But of altruistic ecstasy at the prospect not of cash- but soul-
Savings, rescuing the imperilled spirits of a lumpenproletariat
Just before they tipped over the precipice of ethical
Incapacity into the belching pits of flaming Hellfare
(Into which the tax-paying *'precariat'* may themselves tip
At any time) – these salivating soul-savers scoffing on
Their Wolf fare; while all those who still crow that those long-
Resounding howls have now hollowed out to howling stomachs,
And that *'the wolves which once infested our forests'*
Are returning now in droves and scavenging among the scraps
And bones and Biffa-bins, sniffing for elusive truffles in
The moss and mould collecting between the thinning Trussell trees,
Woefully missing the wood for the wages freeze, clinging
To the long-gone arguments as to the right of *'going on
The Lloyd George', 'the dole'*, the giro, *'the scrounge'*, no,

Those good old bad days have long gone, along with the lounging
Growls of borrow-hood (the wolves are already in the woods!)
And fellowship from the profligate Welsh magician
Of Tŷ Newydd, and all his thriftless followers (other Welshmen
Among them) – and in their place, a new dignity in indigence,
A starving into values, deprivation without relief,
Redemption through compulsory fasting, virtue cultivated
Through mandatory volunteering – now the unemployed
Can lift up their heads and look their God straight in the face,
There's no disgrace in starving… And no doubt Iain Damascus
Smith – ex-axe-man of Caxton House, 'sick snatcher',
Self-proclaimed 'Roman Catholic', in spite of the apostasy
Of his political habits, ripe, surely, for excommunication? –
Is inclined to forget such historical credo on the imperative
Of providing eudemonia for one's fellow humans simply
Because they abjectly lack rudimentary comforts, warmth,
Shelter, raiment, beds and bodily nourishments; but 'IDS'
Would do well to take note of Marcel Mauss's *'Note on alms'*,
From his Apocryphal Gospel, *The Gift*: *'Alms are the fruits*
Of a moral notion of the gift and of fortune on the one hand,
And of a notion of sacrifice, on the other. Generosity
Is an obligation, because Nemesis avenges the poor and
The gods for the superabundance of happiness and wealth
Of certain people who should rid themselves of it. This is
The ancient morality of the gift, which has become a principle
Of justice. The gods and the spirits accept that the share
Of wealth and happiness that has been offered to them
And had been hitherto destroyed in useless sacrifices
Should serve the poor and children' –not so under our
Redeemer Duncan Smith: he's no stomach for filling
Stomachs, only emptying them, for now is the time
To dole out *moral* recompense –for spirits are more
Willing the weaker the flesh, O yea, many famished
Senses have afforded angelic glimpses and light-headed
Raptures! *Praise Him, Praise Him!* – but also to keep their coils
Anchored to this life, at just the right amount of ounces
To weigh down their suspended spiritual cords and militate
Against their lifting up too swift in raptures, trap them in
This Purgatory, coupons for soup-kitchens and food banks

Will be meted out to penitents in transubstantiated rations…
O how self-sacrificing these Tories are, to focus so much
On saving souls by stripping them of benefits, while all the while
Knowing – by dint of their own mostly inherited riches
And gratuities (the accumulative assets of monetarist
Antinomianism), which, as with those they gainfully employ,
They *get to work for them* through shares, investments,
Speculations (no worker in capitalism is more exploited
And put-upon than *money!*) – they themselves will see nothing
Of that very Salvation to which they send so many reformed
Profligates through the spiritual replenishment of imposed
Penury, unless future scientists invent some newfangled
Means by which camels can squeeze through needles' eyes
And the rich get into Heaven, eventually, in ginger groups
Hedging their bets that they can persuade God to privatise…

Sixth Rapture: *Shut Curtains during the Day*

Unlike riches, policies do have a trickledown effect,
And the dictates of Damascus Smith – hairshirt Thomas Malthus
Of Caxton House/or Gregor Mendel of the DWP –
Would germinate into a pearl-white species of cropped
Correspondences in Kafkaesque script bespeaking strange augurs,
Barbed inferences, grim omens, pointed portents – vatic tans
Vibrating with cryptic stings: *'A query has arisen regarding
Your claim…'*, or, *'We are letting you know what might happen to you'*,
But without actually doing so, only adumbrating through
Deliberate ambiguity and mystique of omission (the old
Hemingway tip-of-the-iceberg effect), lacings of uncertainty,
Leaving the door wedged open to auto-suggestion, taxing
Anxious imaginations prone to catastrophic projections –
The implicatures captured uniquely in tan paper raptures;
While elliptic and ecliptic occupational purposes, strange
Occulting ranks and titles, Customer Compliance Officers,
Brought thoughts of Thought Police or plain-clothed
Gestapo in tan macs with glacial stares behind impenetrable
Spectacles turning up on doorsteps clutching rolled umbrellas
And black leather briefcases stuffed full with thumbscrews,
Coat-hangers, piano wires, tape-recorders and lie-detectors –
While Government encouragement of neighbourly petit-
Espionage on unemployed suspects (more the 'Big *Brother*
Society') upped the tan ante for vigilante attitudes
And raised the temperature spiking the thunderous atmosphere
To puncture-point as Ministers instructed conscientious
Citizens to take note of those windows with *'shut curtains
During the day'* – or, in Baronet Osborne's vocabulary:
'Closed shutters' – as they left for work each morning: dawn
Patrols of resentful workers directed to mark front doors
Of suspected Dole-Judes, like so many beady-eyed jackdaws –
It's a peculiarly English kind of malice that criminalises
Innocents and victimises victims of circumstances thrust
On them by others' *'tough choices'* and *'difficult decisions'*…
How appropriate that the Department for War on the Poor
Should send out such vindictive missives in envelopes
Of various browns, parcelling captured sunlight

To disinfect the disaffected, frightened, forgotten, pilloried,
Persecuted, tarred-and-feathered benefit spendthrifts
And profligates, scapegoats and targets for the ran-tan tanning
Of stigmatising tans – what strange types of *benefits* that grant
No benefits, neither to wallet nor wellbeing, but only
Deplete peace of mind and suppress appetites of 'useless eaters',
'Asocial' and 'arbeitsscheu' – is that part of the point, to soften
The blow of swallowed-up cash-flow by shrinking stomachs
So there's less need for food but more room for souls to grow
Like tapeworms of purely spiritual appetites distending
Themselves on the carroty acid reflux of phantom
Mastication, swishing round in rapturous backwashes from
Half-digested papers…? Some recipients experience
Epiphanies: eat the tan envelopes, as if they were unleavened
Victuals, bellies booming out with brown Holy Ghosts…

Seventh Rapture: *Plantagenet Spring*

Others might protest, attempt to fight for some right
To dignity and digestible foods since they did not choose
To fall on hard times – though today there is less opportunity
For group uprisings for we are estranged from our neighbours
(Especially by petit-espionage encouraged among some
With the unkindness of strangers), as from our classes
(Stratified transparencies), nor do we have any bargaining
Powers as in bygone ages, as after the Black Death that laid
Waste to these islands, almost a third of the population
Depleted by its spread – in spite of the best efforts of beak
Doctors whose pecking nosecones were filled with camphor,
Myrrh, cloves, ambergris, balm-mint leaves, laudanum and
Rose – thus a sudden labour shortage, nobles' demand for
Peasants to till their lands soon outstripping supplies, so
The serfs, who had up until then *'only owned their bellies'*,
Suddenly found they now owned scarcer commodities:
Their limbs and hands – and this knowledge brought its own
Demands, not simply for parsimonious wage increases,
But for a more equitable playing field for labour, freedom
For the worker to choose his employer, an end to the rigid
Feudal structure, but above all else a growing refusal
Among the poorer to bow to the poll-tax collector,
Especially among the radicalised Men of Kent, famous for
Their recalcitrance, spurred on by Wat Tyler, Captain
Of their Common Cause, an army never seen before,
An army of peasants armed with scythes and pitchforks,
Tramping in *'ragged angry rhythms'* all the way to Smithfield
On stomachs sloshing with frumenty and ruminants
Of John Ball's frothing sermons, broth of revolt spiced
With sedge and sage by this fierce Hedge Priest, hearts lifted
With Wat Tyler's fulminations, to beat their beatitudes
Straight in the milk-white face of green Richard Plantagenet
(The Second), still wet behind the ears up until the moment
He betrayed them – but in spite of defeat, a signal for change
Grew stronger through the ages, thanks to that radical,
Unabashed, famished army clad in browns and umbers –
And to buboes, unlikely liberators of those swart peasants

Left behind after the pitiless *atra mors* had snatched up
A mighty third of Christendom in Black raptures – a pandemic
That changed the map forever, more conspicuous than today's
Brown Death which claims more marginal demographics,
Pouches of pocket communities less easy to spot,
For it's a more targeted plague that nibbles away at the fringes,
Depicted as moral leprosy, *'scrounger'* germ, *'scrounger'* contagion…

Eighth Rapture: *Kerygma & Seisaktheia*

For brown has ever been the colour of poverty, plainness,
Humbleness, the rustic, humility, peasantry, pauperism –
The colour worn by Francis of Assisi, patron saint of the poor,
Whose Order wore brown in honour of his mission,
Those Franciscan friars who forewent worldly goods,
Opted out to hoboism, tromping pilgrimages *'rag-glad*
In gowns of grey-russet' – thus wrote William Langland in *Piers*
Plowman, an illuminated manuscript painstakingly scrolled
By monkish calligraphic scribes; and today those brown robes
Are re-emerging into the scorching light of a June day
In Twenty-Fourteen, tramping London's sun-pounded,
Empurpled tarmac streets in a march against austerity,
A placard-carrying pilgrimage of practical Christianity
No longer content to brood in caliginous glooms and
Cloistered cools of flagstones and porches, but compelled
To add their voices to a vital counter-narrative
To new Roman yokes of forward-combed Tories in togas,
Regimes of lictors castigating the poor with carrot-less
Sticks and hounding out the state-orphaned Children
Of Doledea, the new 'Jews', the Welfare Jews; these Left-
Feeling Faithful follow in the footsteps of the new Pope
Who calls himself 'Francis' and proclaims his Church *'for*
The poor' (at a time when no one else is for them), throwing
Open the Pact of the Catacombs to the Light in opposition
To the Capitalist Pilates – Markets, Troika and Procurators
Of Ponzi pyramid scams on democracies – who wash their hands
Of responsibility for the welfare of those they exploit
Or render destitute – Captains of Austerity; Pope Francis
Publishes his Apostolic Exhortation, his edict for
Inclusion of the poor, contrapuntal to persecutions
By Pontius Pilate politicians and spurious distinctions
Between *'deserving/undeserving poor'*... *'As long as the problems*
Of the poor are not radically resolved by rejecting
The absolute autonomy of markets and financial
Speculation and by attacking the structural causes
Of inequality, no solution will be found for the world's
Problems or... any problems. Inequality is the root

Of social ills'; this Pope has the spiritual spine to call
Capitalism *'poison'*, *'a tyranny'*, to argue austerity
Is theft from the poor, *'Not to share wealth with the poor is
To steal'* it from them; argues for *'nourishment'*, a *'dignified
Sustenance'* and *'temporal welfare and prosperity'*,
Calls for authenticity so workers might be the *'artisans
Of their destiny'*; accuses Capitalism of perpetrating
A Satanic Pact of oppression and mass pauperisation
For the profits of the few – diagnoses the phantom construct
Of Adam Smith: *'We can no longer trust in the unseen forces
And the invisible hand of the market'* (no, for it only deals
In sleight-of-hand); this Pope calls for a new *kerygma*
In place of stigma for the impoverished, just as, in Ancient
Greece, Solon the Lawgiver called for *Seisaktheia*, debt-wipe,
A shaking off of burdens – not a shaking off of *the burdened*,
As has come to pass under monetarist austerity;
Like all prophets, spiritual and social, before him – Solon,
Christ, Aquinas, Winstanley, Saint-Simon, Comte, Paine,
Owen, Marx, Smillie, Keir Hardie, Nye Bevan – Pope
Francis calls for a change of mind and heart, *'The creation
Of a new mindset which thinks in terms of community
And the priority of the life of all over the appropriation
Of goods by a few'* – more Socialist Republic than Big Society,
Now we've not only red vicars and archbishops but also
A Red Pope and leftwing Franciscans; so spoke Brother
Robert in the thick of scorched protest along with his
Fellow friars: *'Christianity places a quite firm obligation
From those who have more to share to look after those who have less'* …
Just as Christ said: *'Go and give all thou hast to the poor'*…Something
Long forgotten by Tory apostates, now their tight-fisted,
Grasping breed won't even give the benefit of the doubt
Of an abandoned doorway, nor shelter of properties left empty,
Only prison cells courtesy of Weatherley's *'Leave 'Em Out In All
Weathers'* Law, or beds of metal studs on window-ledges outside
Tesco stores: alfresco iron maidens, knobbly blunt instruments
To nudge *at* wingless spines, puncture anthropomorphic pigeons…

Ninth Rapture: *Saint Gemma & Saint Walter*

And of the brown spectrum as well as the taupe and sepia
Tones of heavenward-gazing Gemma Galgani, *'Daughter
Of Passion'*, Patron Saint of the Unemployed (and pharmacists,
In her native Italy, but also of the world) captured
In photographic rapture, caught up with angelic visions
In impoverishment, marked with stigmata at twenty-one,
And finally snatched up after months of spluttering consumption,
Ruptured lungs, on Holy Saturday, 1903, aged just
Twenty-five – up until which age, today, the hounded young
May soon no more have the right to make a claim to the state
For alms to give them shelter, for St. Gemma's beneficiaries
Are punctually stigmatised as apprentice parasites simply
For not being in employment, education, training or 'voluntary'
Enslavement, temporarily, at any given time – at eighteen,
Granted the right to vote, to drive, to drink, or to die for
Their country, but no more the right to have the rent met
On one-bedroom flats, studios, rooms, lodgings, grottos,
Hovels, bedsits, while they try to find occupations to pay
Their way and take up places in a society which doesn't wish
To take them up, and which strips them of any entitlements
At all up to five-and-twenty – lest they be among the prolific
Casualties in the epidemic Malthusian Plague that sweeps
The land as a penny-pinching pestilence, fiscal Locusts
Intent on carrying away the surplus population of economic
Cripples, to snatch them up in raptures of Tan Death
The sunlight-cleansing sickness of a Tan Age augmented
By perma-tanned MPs; and, as if it hasn't happened many
Times before, government campaigns to put the unemployed
To the thrash of a mass tanning, until the maps of surplus
Populations are saturated in spilt tans, those able-bodied
Persons who have idleness and poverty stamped upon them
By collapsing Capitalism, made examples of, exploited
For slave labour in work rehabilitation camps, whipped
Into submission and the rhythm of rocks, to split stones
Like atoms – they had at least a champion, once, in 'Wal'
Hannington, 'St. Walter', priceless polemicist, campaigner,

And leader of the oxymoronic National Unemployed
Workers Movement, in the Thirties, who exposed the punishing
Nature of social services schemes, shamed Stanley Baldwin's
'Break 'em in with boulders' dignity-grinding regime…

Tenth Rapture: *Brown Ominous*

All hail the ragged glad, the angry glad, the rag-tag with black
Gangrened feet tied in tan paper bags, tramps, vagrants,
Beggars, gypsies, travellers, 'Wrags' all raked out and scattered
With the Caxton tans, the flagellating tans – the little tan
Savage gods: small paper packets of black-inked seeds
Which gradually germinate stigmas and memes, mind-tendrils
Of strange detergent urges to rinse out the oesophagus, or
Sprout into nooses, even among claimants of sounder minds,
Since all are cursed with Sisyphus prescriptions, rumours
Of black spots to top up brown studies to brownouts,
Origami thought-forms sprouting from poisonous printing inks,
Paper folded sharp as guillotines or portcullises,
Correspondences of purposeful crossed-purposes cropped
To prickle phobic consciences popped off by proxy
To cap unemployment figures; ominous brown windows
Of howling shibboleths (even more ominous when they
Come in beige or isabelline: those are the Atos albatrosses
Beating their wings of bounty incentives) which, once spoken,
Open up impecunious sesames and cans of worms
While simultaneously shutting curtains on claimants
After defenestration without witnesses – the final
Triangulation for slow strangulation – and this is part
Of the sport for tan harpies, tan snatchers, tan accusers,
Kangaroo judges and juries, snatching tans that snatch away
Securities then grab the giro-souls of those driven
To suddenly ending their claims prematurely, signing off
From life for terror of *'error'*, at threat of interrogations,
Sanctions, prosecutions, dispossessions, denied burial
On consecrated grounds of *'hardworking taxpayers'*;
Surreptitiously depleted from DWP spreadsheets;
Or those who 'disappear', simply shrink away for visceral fear
Of brown envelopes – now recognised as a psychological
Disorder in its' own right to be slipped in the onion-skinned
DSM, ripe opportunity for pharmaceutical pill-
Cutters to profit from by coming up with another new
Wonder drug; *'Brown Envelope Syndrome'* (BES), sometimes
Nicknamed *'Brown Terrors'*, *'Beige Ague'*, or *'Antsy Tans'*,

Can display symptoms normally associated with delirium
Tremens: shaky hands, clammy palms and hallucinations
Of tans on the doormat even on those days when they are
Absent (*'tan hallucinations'*); while otherwise *'Brown Terror'*
Has all the classic hallmarks of anxiety – hence its' other
Sobriquets: *'Tan Angst', 'Tan Panic', 'Tan Anxiety', 'Tan
Terror'* – O those ENV 27s that traverse the convoluted
Veins and tortuous arteries of the mollusc-slow postal
System, twenty-four-seven; Byzantian tans that sliver round
The houses circuitously before arriving and visiting
Their plagues on shivering receivers, so many innocent
Orestes nonetheless in the throes of hot pursuit by vicious
Missives of sulphur-hissing prose sent hurtling like flaming
Arrows from bows of fulminating buff Furies – ominous
Browns, scourge of lumpen unemployed papyrophobes…

Eleventh Rapture: *Dutch Caps*

But, to Janus-faced Smith, Pharisaic Saul of Whitehall,
Tan envelopes are passports to hope, salvation missives,
And his Acts, the cleansings of souls denied sunlight for too long,
Left on the parasite-infested scrapheap of benefits,
To perish, but not before reproducing dependents,
Profligate offspring; hence Herod Smith announced
No more support for any third child born to unemployed
Parents – a Capping of the Innocents; but for those more
Recalcitrant couples, refuseniks of fiscal restraint who
Persist in intimacies without French Letters of introduction
(And this also applies to couples where only one partner is
Unemployed – the less talked-about taboo of claimant and
Non-claimant miscegenation, which carries a fifty per cent
Risk of passing on the *'scrounger'* gene), or are unresponsive
To vulcanised rubber, or those whose Roman Catholic
Scruples preclude more Protestant pro-choice options,
But continue to irresponsibly procreate and fly in the face
Of the Welfare State's gentrification, those non-contributory
Mothers will find they've brought foundlings without state-
Entitlements howling into an unforgiving England,
Since now the benefit system has *'Gone Dutch'* (along
With pensions) at the behest of hard-pressed taxpayers
Who only have babies if they can afford to, so prudent,
Presuming the nappies and extra food can be absorbed
Into projected budgets, or accommodated one pram
At a time – otherwise, Dutch caps are the best family
Planners (*'There's no benefit cap as foolproof as a Dutch cap!*
Specially lubricated with a spermicidal gel formulated to repel
The most 'scrounger'-prone of sperms!' might go the strap-line –
Free Dutch caps in DWP starter packs, so now
The unemployed can have their raptures nappy-free! Or,
What more appropriate patron than *Rapture* contraceptives);
So those third children discouraged while still in the womb
Will be born into post-natal ostracism with the cutting
Of the umbilical *'broo'*, and will be up against
The wrought-iron gates of the poorhouse from day one,
Lots of Lowryesque stick-like Oliver Twists, Little Father

Times (Junior Judes), witnessing remorseless punishments
Heaped on their parents for sins against society – sins
Which *are* the children – at ages dangerously young,
The pawning of furniture to pay impossible rents,
The queuing up at food banks, the permanent temporary
Limbos of B&Bs – one can only shudder at those future
Coupon-sponsored shadow-orphans of conditionality
Fainting in classrooms for vitamin-sapped lack of stamina,
Dragged up in damp rooms nourishing only mould,
Cribbed in obscurity, weaned on tinned *Carnation*,
Whittled into stigmatised, guilt-ridden gnomes by
The scything knives of selective poverty; and some,
Through a strange strangled sense of duty without
Instructions, seeing themselves as problems, computing
Curious equations only fathomable to those with a shortage
Of omega and vitamins as knights move abstractions,
In the absence of National Insurance number eligibilities,
And morally recognised identities, that they're just burdens,
Obsoletes, botched abortions best throttled-off in cots,
Dead weights – and so, accordingly, tie knots around
Their throats – and, if they have any younger siblings,
Press pillows softly on their snoring mouths – then go
A-dangling, leaving behind scrawled notes elucidating
Antic gestures of chilling juvenile logic: *'Done because
The State says we are too menny'*; though when push comes
To shove-ha'penny the door remains ajar to optional
Denouements: the redemptive Dickens or damnatory Hardy…

Twelfth Rapture: *Sunlight is the Best Disinfectant*

But to our rich deciders, Guardians in gratuity,
Any fate is better than the pit of poverty, and, opposite
To the intention of its invention, the Welfare State mutated
Into another means for trapping people in the poverty
It was supposed to help them escape, for benefits have never
Really benefited anyone, at least, not in the rug-pulled-
From-under-them long-run (nor, it seems, the short-term);
In spite of beneficent intent and being *'far too generous'*
(Almost up to the point, sometimes, of brushing subsistence!
But not quite, kept just beneath it to so as not to incentivise
Voluntary worklessness – was ever Beveridge's template),
'It's not moral or Christian' to keep the unemployed in
Spiritual emptiness (thus the crucial intercessions of tan
Raptures!) – better to have them purge impecunious corruptions
Through mandatory fasting, alleviated unevenly by
A scavenging of vouchers snatched up by ravenous hands,
But nothing must interrupt the dismantlement of apparatus
Put in place by those past pilots of moral irresponsibility
Who interpreted their Scriptures as practical templates
From which to construct a compassionate bureaucracy
(To Tories, Christianity is entirely an aesthetic feature,
Quaint ornament to charm the idle daydreaming mind,
A figurative Gothic folly in a plunging Darwinian garden,
Nothing more), altruistic structure of Social Security –
The Welfare State: *This*, the kind sin of Clement Attlee
The Prelate, and Evangelist Nye Bevan – a regenerating
Organism of evergetism grown from social Gospels,
A Jerry-built Jerusalem sprouted from arable parables,
Prefabricated metaphors and flat-packed aphorisms,
A municipal Parousia of civic miracles and Damascene
Conversions, which stretched Peter's fishing nets tight enough
To catch all the bottom-feeders rather than sifting them out –
The safety net that filtered nothing, until fin-rot set in;
Now it's time for the belated sifting, for liberating indigents
From idleness, lifestyle loafers from thriftless sins,
Now they're all for the snatching up, the carrying away
On tan paper pinions, to be raised up, pulled up by

Their bootstraps, *'not a handout but a hand-up',* up out of giro-
Grouted grottos, handout hovels, mould-spore studios,
Dingy bedsits, lifted up, up on flapping wings of tan ravens –
All will be caught up in the fight-or-flight cathedral-light,
The stained-glass light of tan raptures, contrary answers
To prayers of fag-singed fingers, burnt tan thumbs:
For the Pharisees say *'Sunlight is the best disinfectant…'*

Thirteenth Rapture: *Tan Rapture*

There's a special type of skin that can attract a tan
In the shade of blinds and shutters, a kind of thin translucent
English onion-skin that can catch the sun through shut curtains,
That no darkness can etiolate, but burnishes bronze
Under glaring light-bulbs – such dermatological
Exceptions are more the rule nowadays: most shadow-
Bathers brown themselves in the glooms of rented grottos,
Garrets, attics, studio dark rooms, buffing up like mushrooms,
Most of them, by now, have caught the sun of nocturnal moons,
Lycanthropic scroungers or vampiric parasites –
Take your pick from folkloric dysphemisms; and still more
Are catching tans almost daily through the blinding white
Windows of paper envelopes, pattering tan rectangles
Snatching up one and all, first and last in raptures, or,
For those who still remain, the promise of salvation
With zero hours paid below inflation, or the purgatorial
Grace of underemployment, or limbo of mandatory
Voluntarism, community placements, apprenticeships,
Interminable internships – worship at the altar of Work,
The new Wicca! The curd and the wey, the payday lender,
The weekend bender, the Sunday hangover, the foggy
Monday morning, the grey impersonality of alienated labour –
Unproductive, purely symbolic labour done for its own sake,
But which estranges the worker, even from earning enough
To afford to buy the commodities he himself produces,
What Marx termed in the German *entfremdung* – an estranging
From *Gattungswesen*, the *'species-essence'* (even more so
Today than in his own time, for now the employed are
Depersonalised from their occupational purpose through
The rights-stripping virus of *'zero hours contracts'* – no more
Simply coping with the perennial suppression of personality
In the workplace, pathology for the permanent temp);
Or labour that is of no use to anyone, of no fathomable
Purpose to society: sales, advertising, call centres, public
Relations; purely symbolic labour, symbolic as money
Has become, once a symbol of exchange but now something
In itself, a purely illusory useless something

Of no intrinsic value – and Marx had a term for this too,
'Commodity-fetishism', a quasi-mystical transfiguration
Of commodities, objects, things into animistic material forms
Inspirited by advertising spiel with personalities sporting
Specific traits, thought forms, almost 'beings' in their own rights,
Object-gods, ergonomic demiurges urging us
To buy and worship them in our homes, carpeted shrines –
Personification of product until it appears to have human
Attributes – *'reification'* – while the human producer's stripped,
Depersonalised to a robotic producer of things to consume,
Reduced to an automaton on the factory lines,
Whittled to a *'thing'*, he and his labour commoditised
By industrial magic – worker becomes commodity,
His act of labour, a symbol, while commodity assumes
His deracinated sentience, symbol becomes being –
And this is no more manifest than in advertising Copy
(Thus Edmund Wilson heaped on Marx the epithet *'Poet
Of Commodities'*, a compliment – as opposed to the wholly
Different meaning such a phrase would hold when thrust
On the copywriter – in his polemical monograph,
To the Finland Station)... But for the better-heeled, the City
Stockbroker, banker, hedge-better and speculator, no such
Alienation, and there's always the weekend tailoring binge,
Measuring up for the latest cut of flannel suit from Hugo
Boss's subtropical Gestapo range, replete with crisp tan shirts
And rum-fudge ties; or Dante Zeller's Tuxedo and Menswear
Two-button notch lapel *Tan Rapture* as designed by Jean Yves,
With non-vented besom pockets; and, for the ladies, Scuch's
Line in *Rapture* boots available in plenitudes of tan – such
Are the sartorial raptures of our conspicuously
Consuming *'wealth-creators'*, but nothing can compare
To tan paper raptures visited on unemployed peasants,
Plebs, *hoi polloi* and lumpenproletariat that can take them
Up in smoke unawares, any time, unexpectedly,
Alchemically, their particular rapture tailored to fit
With chalk streaks, bespoke spontaneous consumptions...

Fourteenth Rapture: *Two Types of Brown Envelopes*

In theosophy, tan auras are purported to indicate
Analytical thinkers, the conscientious and thrifty,
While, oppositely, brown auras are associated with
Unethical business, unscrupulousness, cupidity,
Particularly if of a muddy tincture with a smudge of grey,
Like a brown cloud thoughtform (*That's Capitalism!*) –
And the lobbying boys pass round brown paper envelopes
Snapped up by our 'incorruptible' politicians,
Cash for questions, no questions asked, and certainly none
Answered (cue tap of the nose), and when MPs are found
Out they express much shock at their pure stupidity,
Apologise in third person as if on behalf of someone else,
Couch their white-collar crimes as *'mistakes'* no matter
How calculated and transparently perpetrated,
They feign forgetfulness, confusion or aberration,
Grasping at straws for there's no other grain of justification,
Since they have no hardship to blame for succumbing
To temptation – unlike those dole-*'scroungers'* they routinely
Pillory – of making claims for fictitious expenses, flipping
Homes for pecuniary gains, they emphatically go against
The grain of the lion's share of *'honest and hardworking
MPs'*, but it's a grain gone against time and time again
And one after another the grafters are caught out one
And the same for unscrupulous opportunism, contempt
For democracy, abuses of privilege, pissing on
The taxpayers they so often invoke by name, and not least,
The voters, who put them in place to represent them,
A sense of unfettered entitlement, embezzlement in all
But name, parliamentary peccadilloes, professional fraud
There for all to see in the disinfecting sunlight but for
Lack of transparency – then they shuffle through the lobbies
To put crosses by Yeas which push the latest Bill through
Parliament to post tan raptures through letterboxes
Of *'Long-Term Benefits'* (LTBs), or, in Jobcentreplus-ese,
'Lying Thieving Bastards', those Not in Education Employment
Or Training (NEETs), or those souls stuck on the sick,
Most dosed so high on Serotonin Reuptake Inhibitors

In their reclusion, that they are, in any case, sunlight-sensitive
(Which might in part explain those *'curtains shut during the day'*,
Apart from those who work night shifts); yes, they send those
Round robins, brown robins round until the brown owls
Are all browned out or flown away once and for all,
And it'd take a very quick brown fox to jump over the lazy dog,
The lazy scrounging dog that gnaws on its bone idleness
And sucks out the marrow of *'soft-touch'* English kindness
In this beneficent welfare state that is *'too generous'*, yea,
They've never had it so good nor will ever have it good again,
Not by a long chalk – black on racking tans can snatch us up
Unawares at any time, but until such times, the snatching tans
Keep rustling to the protracted clapping of taxpayers' hands…

It's a special opportunity unemployment captures:
To be morally redeemed and snatched up in tan raptures…

Post-Rapture: *A Compromise Too Far*

No canonisation forthcoming for the DWP's Supreme
Decision Maker of the past six years, more damnation
With faint praise for Iain Duncan Smith, architect
Of the bedroom tax, unemployment benefit caps
And sickness cut ups, no matter how much his self-
Proclaimed 'Roman Catholic' claims might covet such,
Though his Tory tribe might respectfully strip him of his pre-
DWP epithet, *'the quiet man of politics'*, laying
Emphasis on his Works on behalf of the centre-right
Centre for Social Justice (more a sociological stalking horse
For Victorian scrub-them-with-carbolic workhouse ethics),
Replace it with the title, Tory Patron Saint of Poverty
Solutions/Self-Appointed Tsar of Insolvency-Solving
(Though IDS would claim divine anointing for such divining):
Solving poverty by simply taking the poor out of the picture,
Wiping as many off the map as possible while damply
Wiping the palimpsest of death stats in the process,
And brushing the remainder under the rhetorical carpet,
Or tipping them out into deeper despair and ruin, depleting
The incapacitated and economically unproductive
Populations by percentages, especially expedient
In the case of the black-triangle-badged *'arbeitsscheu' ('workshy')*,
But, unlike those organised thugs of Thirties Germany
(Who make the likes of Duncan Smith and his henchmen
And women – Grayling, Freud, Miller, McVey – seem mere
Amateur Braunhemden by comparison), not wiping out
The poor from hatred or malice, but wiping them out from
'Compassion'… Smith's resignation on 18 March 2016,
A last ditch gesture to distance himself from an umpteenth
Dumping on the disabled in a cloth-cutting Chancellor's
Six-year fiscal holocaust of the impecunious sick,
Even though Duncan Smith was athletic hatchet-man for
This lap of the Government's gentrified eugenics circuit,
And left his traumatising mark across its moral deficit;
Thought by quitting in synthetic protest against cuts
He drew up himself he might acquit himself in advance
Of the verdict from a U.N. investigation into his abuses

Of disability rights (small wonder he campaigned so
Athletically for a speedy *'Brexit'* so his past department
Could no longer come under the purview of the European
Court of Human Rights); he thought by closing the long
Tattered tan-paper chapter to his despotic six year grip
At the DWP, he might somehow be morally redeemed
In the eyes of a future public retrospective impeachment
Of his crimes against the most vulnerable and disadvantaged
For which he'd be arraigned once his 'dark arts' came
To light after maximum damage had been done – call it
Damage-limitation; in spite of leaving behind tan paper
Trails – like spiritual entrails – of 91,000 plus departed souls,
Of whom countless went prematurely, penalised into post-
Sentience, 2,380 within six weeks of being declared *'fit
For work'* by Atos in the space of just three years… He
Choreographed his flight from office with more than just
A minted hint of opportunism, timed it symbolically for
Subeditors to have sport punning on an immortal omen
Uttered by Shakespearean haruspex: *'Beware the IDS
Of March'*: jumped ships on a *'principle'* (apparently) attempting
To pitch some clear blue water between his suddenly discovered
'Conscience' and the Treasury's impromptu announcement
Of some pruning to Personal Independence Payments (until
The PIPs squeaked!) paid to the physically incapacitated –
Particularly those who needed help toileting – juxtaposed
Against tax cuts for the top 5 per cent; for Duncan Smith
This was *'a compromise too far'* and he could not *'sit passively'*
As Pontius Pilate of the DWP, pinching his nose to more
'Salami-slicing', interminable trimmings to benefits for the most
Vulnerable, now more vulnerable than ever before since his
Own spirit-whittling welfare reforms of a swingeing six years
Of long knives swung through legion lives, a paper-pogrom,
A green-fingered rampage during which he vowed to *'weed
Out the workshy'*, and more gardening besides, trim down
The *'culture of entitlement'* and *'idleness'* – O IDS! Seems
'Salami' Smith had another (last minute) Damascene moment,
His second epiphany amidst the deprived, echoes of tearful
Easterhouse, and now goes up into flight on his bespoke
Raptures of lucrative postprandial speeches… Less Himmler,

More Rommel, after all…? Matters little, his thumbs are
Permanently smudged from the ink blots of black spots
Like Orcs' blood dripped from the spikes of a sprung portcullis,
And he'll continue the way of all Conservative recidivism…
Now scuttles in unshaven, pitbullish, blue collar Mr Crab
To the office left vacant by his vatic, evangelical, fanatical
Acronymic predecessor, but he's just as prompt a proselytiser
For the Protestant Sweatshop Ethic, sending press releases
To the *Express* so it can announce in elephantine typeface
MORE CUTS TO CRUTCHED SCROUNGERS, particularly
Those slung in the 'Wrag' like used dishrags, prey of private
Sector wolves in sheep's clothing, packs of Capacity Scouts
For Wolf Cubs, all fangs and paper forms, woofers at the heels
Of the Tory Wolf of *'welfare reform'* – *What's the time, Mr.
Wolf? TIME LIMITED! Time to 'wean' the welfare cubs and
'Useless eaters' off the Wolf-teats of the Welfare State...* for stubbly
Crabb claims he understands the salvific function of Work
(That barking answerback to everything); that Employment
Performs empirical miracles, having witnessed his long-term
Unemployed mother convert – eventually – to its curative
Auspices, pace Damascene, realising a new esteem in
Underpaid exploitation, the glad indignity of *entfremdung* –
No doubt his mum's so proud to see her council estate-raised
Son grown up into a Conservative MP, and now appointed
Sharp-suited Puppet of State for the DWP, not such
A novice vatic, few have doubts as to his copper-bottomed
Stomach for keeping tans rustling to the rapturous applause
Of taxpayers' hands, and for those who just won't get blunt
Instrument 'hints' of sanctions and penalties for disprivilege,
It'll be many trips to the pawnbrokers, food banks, soup kitchens,
And, beyond, rough sleeping with municipal acupunctures
Of homeless spikes, despair, or more permanent departures…

*…for it's a special opportunity that unemployment captures:
To be morally rehabilitated – snatched up in tan raptures…*

Addendum: BENEDICTIONS

*We pray for those tan martyrs so far accounted for
Who sacrificed themselves for the sake of cash-strapped taxpayers...*

Elaine Lowe, 53, COPD; Paul Reekie, 48, depression;
Leanne Chambers, 30, depression; Tim Salter, 53, blind,
Agoraphobic; Carl Payne, 42, father of two; Edward Jacques,
47, HIV, Hepatitis C, depression, self-harm; Steven Cawthra,
55; John Walker, 57; Jacqueline Harris, 53, could hardly walk;
Richard Sanderson, 44; David Barr, 28, mental difficulties;
Nicholas Peter Barker, 51, semi-paralysed; Mark & Helen
Mullins, 48 & 59, fatigued, despairing at daily plodding
To the food bank; Paul Willcoxsin, 33, mental health problems
TOOK THEMSELVES UP IN TAN RAPTURES
Martin Rust, 36, schizophrenic; Craig Monk, 43, partial
Amputee; Lee Robinson, 39; George Scollen, age unknown;
Peter Hodgson, 49, stroke, brain haemorrhage, fused leg;
Sandra Louise Moon, 57, degenerative back condition,
Depression, anxiety; Christopher Charles Harkness, 39,
Mental health issues; Michael McNicholas, 34, severely
Depressed; Victor Cuff, 59, severe depression; Wayne Grew,
37, severe depression; David Elwyn Hughs Harries, 48
TOOK THEMSELVES UP IN TAN RAPTURES
Charles Barden, 74, for fear of the bedroom tax; Iain Hodge,
30, life-threatening Hughes Syndrome; Shaun Pilkington,
58, unable to cope; Chris MaGuire, 61, depression;
Carl Joseph Foster-Brown, 58; Miss DE, early 50s, mental illness;
Ian Jordan, 60, Barratt's Oesophagus; Stuart Holley, 23;
Michael Connolly, 60, father of one; Trevor Drakard, 50,
Severe epileptic; Martin Hadfield, 20, too proud to claim benefits
TOOK THEMSELVES UP IN TAN RAPTURES...
...As did Elaine Christian, 57, by drowning herself, having
Already inflicted ten wounds to her wrists; and Christelle
Pardoe, 32, pregnant, by jumping from a third floor balcony
Whilst clutching her baby son, Kayjah; and Stephanie Bottrill,
53, by walking in front of a lorry for being unable
To afford an extra £80 a month for the bedroom tax
In spite of cutting her costs by living on tinned custard...

*And we pray for all those so far accounted for who were snatched
Up in tan raptures...*

Terry McGarvey, 48, dangerously ill from polycytheamia,
SNATCHED UP IN TAN RAPTURES the day after
His work capability assessment; Mark Wood, 44,
Complex mental health problems, SNATCHED UP IN
TAN RAPTURES through starvation; Karen Sherlock,
44, multiple health issues, SNATCHED UP IN TAN
RAPTURES by a heart attack a month after being found
'Fit for work'; Linda Wootton, 49, a double heart and
Lung transplant, SNATCHED UP IN TAN RAPTURES
Nine days after Atos found her 'fit for work'; Elenore Tatton,
39, SNATCHED UP IN TAN RAPTURES weeks after
Being found 'fit for work'; Brian McArdle, 57, SNATCHED
UP IN TAN RAPTURES after a fatal heart attack the day
After his disability benefits were stopped; Stephen Hill,
53, SNATCHED UP IN TAN RAPTURES by a heart attack
One month after being found 'fit for work'; David Groves,
56, SNATCHED UP IN TAN RAPTURES by a heart attack
The night before taking his work capability assessment;
Colin Traynor, 29, epilepsy, SNATCHED UP IN TAN
RAPTURES after being stripped of his benefits, winning
His appeal posthumously five weeks later; Mark Scott,
46, SNATCHED UP IN TAN RAPTURES after his
Benefits were stopped; Cecilia Burns, 51, found 'fit for work'
While undergoing treatment for breast cancer, SNATCHED
UP IN TAN RAPTURES just a few weeks after she won
Her appeal against the Atos decision; Chris Cann, 57,
SNATCHED UP IN TAN RAPTURES just months after
Being told he had to undergo a medical assessment
To prove he couldn't work; Larry Newman, degenerative
Lung condition, weight dropped to 7 stone, SNATCHED UP
IN TAN RAPTURES after Atos awarded him zero points;
Paul Turner, 52, SNATCHED UP IN TAN RAPTURES
From ischaemic heart disease, having been told to find a job
After a heart attack; David Coupe, 57, a cancer sufferer
Found 'fit for work' by Atos: lost his sight, then his hearing,
Then his mobility, then his life – *UP IN TAN RAPTURES;*

Ian Caress, 43, multiple health issues, deteriorating
Eyesight, SNATCHED UP IN TAN RAPTURES ten months
After being found 'fit for work' by Atos – his family
Described his corpse resembling a concentration camp victim's;
Kevin Bennett, 40, schizophrenia, virtual recluse after
Having his benefits stopped, found dead in his flat having
Been SNATCHED UP IN TAN RAPTURES; Denis Jones,
58, disabled, SNATCHED UP IN TAN RAPTURES after
Being hit by the bedroom tax; Paul ?, 51, found dead in
A freezing cold flat after his ESA was stopped, his appeal found
In his favour on the day he was SNATCHED UP IN TAN
RAPTURES; Peter Duut, Dutch national with terminal cancer,
SNATCHED UP IN TAN RAPTURES leaving behind
A destitute widow unable to afford a funeral for him;
Julian Little, 47, wheelchair-bound, suffering kidney failure,
Lost his essential dialysis room due to the bedroom tax,
SNATCHED UP IN TAN RAPTURES; Robert Barlow, 47,
Brain tumour, a heart defect and awaiting a transplant, deemed
'Fit for work' by Atos, his benefits withdrawn, SNATCHED
UP IN TAN RAPTURES penniless less than two years later;
Annette Francis, 30, mum-of-one with severe mental illness,
SNATCHED UP IN TAN RAPTURES after her disability
Benefits were ceased; Janet McCall, 53, terminally ill
With pulmonary fibrosis, declared 'fit for work' by Atos
And the DWP, SNATCHED UP IN TAN RAPTURES
5 months after her benefits were stopped; Graham Shawcross,
63, debilitating Addison's disease, SNATCHED UP IN TAN
RAPTURES by cardiac arrest after an Atos 'fit for work' decision;
David Clapson, 59, diabetic ex-soldier deprived of the means
To keep his insulin chilled, half-starved, SNATCHED UP
IN TAN RAPTURES; Chris Smith, 59, terminal cancer,
SNATCHED UP IN TAN RAPTURES just as he was declared
'Fit for work' by Atos; Nathan Hartwell, 36, SNATCHED UP
IN TAN RAPTURES by heart failure on his birthday, after
An 18-month battle with the DWP; Jan Mandeville, 52,
Fibromyalgia, driven to the point of mental and physical
Breakdown, after battling the DWP for ESA and DLA,
SNATCHED UP IN TAN RAPTURES TAN RAPTURES
TAN RAPT SNATCHED RAPTURES SAP PATCHED

*SNATCHERS SNAP PATCHERS TRAP CURES SATURE
NAP TARES RATS PURE TAP SPARE PASTURES UP
RAPTURES*

Notes

Digger Hinges
In 2012 a rural offshoot of the urban Occupy Movement, calling themselves the Runnymede Diggers, set up a tent-camp just off the campus of Brunel University near Runnymede, in an attempt to replicate the Digger communes of 1648-50; as with their 17th century harbingers, they were predictably evicted.
Lackland: derogatory sobriquet given to King John (1199-1216) for his having 'lost' England its territories in Normandy.
Capotains: tall-crowned, narrow-brimmed, hats worn by men and women from the 1590s to the mid-17th c.
Gerrard Winstanley: (1609-1676) visionary figurehead of the Diggers and author of many polemical pamphlets.
John Lilburne: (1614-1657) the pamphleteering figurehead the Levellers, who campaigned for male suffrage and a 'levelling' of the land (i.e. equalising of rights).
Diggers: an egalitarian movement of 1648-59 which, in a protest against private property and through a biblical conviction that the earth was to share in common, set up camps throughout the country where they attempted to live in common tilling (or digging – thus their name) unused land and growing their own crops to sustain themselves; all such communities were violently evicted by Cromwell's troops.
Cobham, Wellingborough and Iver: the most successful Digger communities.
Brackenborough: surname of the spokesperson for the Runnymede Diggers.
Rainsborough, Goodgroome, Everard: 17th century Levellers.

The Moving Rainbow
See Louise Raw, *Striking a Light: The Bryant and May Matchwomen and their Place in History* (Continuum, 2011).
Phossy-jaw: necrosis of the jaw caused by exposure to phosphorous, as in old match production.
Sesquisulphide: a sulphide that contains three atoms of sulphur in the molecule.
Usufruct: the legal right of using and enjoying the fruits or profits of something belonging to another.
Swedish Match: famous Stockholm-based manufacturer of matches, snuff and chewing tobacco, in *Jönköping* ('City of the matches'); it merged with *Bryant & May* in 1927.
Clementina Black: Brighton-born writer and union activist, honorary secretary of the Women's Trade Union League (1886).

Kata Dalström: 19th c. Swedish campaigner for women's working rights.
Madame Blavatsky: Helena Petrovna von Hahn (1831-91), a 19th c. medium, occultist, clairvoyant and co-founder of the Theosophical Society.

Down the Rainbow Sliding

Jason Gurney: sculptor, Spanish Civil War volunteer.
Clem Beckett: Communist Party member, motorcycle racer and volunteer for the International Brigades in Spain.
Wintringham: (Tom), writer, journalist, poet, co-founder of the *Daily Worker*, and commander of British Battalion, International Brigade.
Sinfield: (George) General Secretary of the British Workers' Sports Federation and *Daily Worker* sports correspondent.
Rust: (William) editor of *Daily Worker*.

Olvido Verde – Olives Bleed Green

In 1975, on the death of the dictator General Franco, the newly elected democratic government of Spain agreed with the Spanish Parliament to proclaim an *el pacto de Olvido*, a 'Pact of Forgetting', whereby there would be no recriminations or post mortems of the suspected atrocities committed in the Spanish Civil War (1936-39), nor of the infringements of human rights perpetrated under the subsequent 36-year Franco dictatorship.
Duchess of Atholl: Scottish Tory politician and social campaigner.
Hyperkulturemia: 'excess of kultur (culture) in the blood', also known as Stendhal syndrome or Florence syndrome, is a psychosomatic state of heightened visual stimulus, sometimes involving panic symptoms and hallucinations, triggered by exposure to too intense and detailed artistic and architectural beauty.
David Gascoyne: (1916-2001) British surrealist poet.
G.D.H. Cole: (1889-1959), socialist, political theorist and prolific author and polemicist.
Nancy Cunard: (1896-1965), writer and political activist.

Red Generals

Rupert John Cornford: (1915-1936) English poet and Communist student leader at Cambridge. He was killed in the early months of the Spanish Civil War Fascism.
Esmond Romilly: (1918-41), British socialist and anti-fascist.
Margot Heinemann: (1913-92), British Marxist writer and scholar.

The Abandoned Shade

Laurie Lee: (1914-1997) English poet; the third volume of his autobiography, *A Moment of War*, describes his time in Spain with the International Brigades.

Greeks Bearing Gifts
This poem was originally written a couple of years before Syriza's victory in the snap election in January 2015, the historic *'Oxi'* (*'No'*) vote of the Greeks against the Troika in July 2015, the new austerity measures imposed by the Troika.

Kleisthenes: founder of Athenian democracy circa 508/7 BC. Draco: (7th c BC), a morally authoritarian legislator/tyrant of Ancient Athens whose strict moral code was particularly severe, hence the term *draconian, 'severe' or 'cruel'*.

Lacedaemonians: Spartans.

Alkibiades: ancient Athenian statesman and orator notorious for switching allegiances from Athens to Sparta, Sparta to Persia, then back to Athens, during the Peloponnesian War; he was eventually assassinated.

Hoplites: citizen soldiers of ancient Greek states drawn from the ranks of free farmers and artisans.

Seisaktheia: 'the shaking off of burdens': policy of national debt-wipe which freed debt-bonded Athenian peasant sharecroppers (*Thetes*) from economic enslavement, instigated by *Solon* (638-558 BC), statesman, poet, reformer and first lawgiver of Athens.

douleia: debt-bondage/debt-slavery in ancient Athens, possibly the etymological root of dole.

kleptocracy: rule by thieves/theft.

timocracy: rule by property-owners.

Peisistratids: three tyrants of Athens reigning between 546 and 510 BC, named after Peisistratus, the paternal first.

Wolfsangels: German heraldic charge/symbol resembling a wolf trap.

Siegfried: hero from Germanic folklore.

Parsifal: hero from Arthurian myth.

Fustanella: skirt-like garment worn by men in the Balkans.

Evzones: elite Greek light infantry.

Symplegades: the 'crashing rocks' through which the Argo had to navigate.

Carpocratians: followers of the 2nd c. Christian Gnostic philosopher, Carpocrates.

The Green Heart of Germany
Landtag: 'assembly of a federated German state.
Landgraves: 'dukes' of the Holy Roman Empire.
Heraldic terms –
   gules: red;
   mullets: stars;
   argent: silver/white;
   azure: blue;
   barry: horizontal stripes;
   rampant: rearing up;
   vert: green.

When is a Red Swede a Beetroot?
Industrial Workers of the World: (IWW), an international radical workers union founded in 1905, their pioneering model of workplace democracy, termed the *'Wobbly Shop'*, led to their nickname, the *'Wobblies'*.
Joe Hill (aka Joseph Hillstrom: (1879-1915): IWW activist and song-writer, framed on a murder charge and executed.
Wal Hannington: (1896-1966), founding member of the Communist Party of Great Britain, National Organiser of the National Unemployed Workers' Movement.

Thaxted Redux
Curtmantle: (from French *court-manteau*), sobriquet of Henry II, probably alluding to his short stature.

Wootton Bassett
Bluemantle: Bluemantle Pursuivant of Arms in Ordinary is a junior officer of (heraldic) arms of the College of Arms in London.
Wrag: acronym for *'Work-Related Activity Group'*, one of the two claimant groups of Employment and Support Allowance (ESA), the other being the Support Group.

Taser Dawn
The Irish traveller communities at a partly legal Dale Farm encampment in Essex were violently evicted by Basildon Council via a dawn raid of taser-armed police in 2011.
Morions: helmets from the 16th and 17th c.
Thurible: metal censer suspended from chains in which incense is burned during Catholic masses.

Ash Friday
Written in support of the Whitechapel Freedom Press Bookshop which was firebombed in the small hours of 1 February 2013.

Thatcher's Statue
Novensides: collective deities regarded by the Romans as foreign imports to their own religion.
Poor doors: nickname given to shabbier side or back-street entrances to residential buildings (particularly in London) for poorer tenants, in contrast to the more salubrious main entrances for the richer occupants.

Glossolalia
Glossolalia: speaking in tongues, a vocal phenomenon thought to represent the original universal language (of God) pre-Babel, sometimes witnessed in evangelical Christian gatherings, though psychiatry deems it a possible symptom of schizophrenia/psychosis.
Ambages: roundabout, indirect ways of saying or doing things.
Strawberry Thieves alludes to the William Morris wallpaper design, *Strawberry Thief*; but it is also the name of a modern day socialist choir.
Bill Brand and Nigel Barton: Bill Brand (1976) was a television series by Trevor Griffiths about a left-wing Labour MP at odds with parliamentary politics; *Stand Up, Nigel Barton and Vote, Vote, Vote for Nigel Barton* (1965/6) were two TV plays by Dennis *Potter* about the political compromises of an initially idealistic working-class Labour MP.
Ewan MacColl: (1915-1989) prolific folk singer-songwriter, actor, poet, communist and Labour activist, who pioneered the 'radio-ballad' form which comprised proletarian social document, poetry and music around social and industrial themes.
Kevin Brownlow and Andrew Mollo: polemical film-makers whose films include *It Happened Here* and *Winstanley*.
Boys from the Blackstuff: tv drama series by Liverpudlian playwright Alan Bleasdale about intermittently unemployed tarmac-layers fighting for survival in Thatcher's Britain.

Orwell Mansions
Une nation de boutiquiers: depiction of England at the end of the 18th century by Bertrand Barère de Vieuzac, although the epithet is often attributed to Napoleon Bonaparte.

Coventry Blue
Domine, dirige nos: motto of the City of London Corporation.
Rhinomacer: a type of word-boring beetle.
Remembrancer: the City of London Corporation's parliamentary agent who sits opposite the Speaker at the other end of the chamber in the House of Commons.
Liberal buff-coloured moths: the original colours of the Liberal Party were blue and buff.
Shadbellies: Regency-style riding coats still worn at some public schools.
Catercaps: 'Canterbury caps', of medieval design, still worn by some female Oxford undergraduates instead of mortarboards.
Reeve: an Anglo-Saxon agent of the King and/or medieval English manor officer responsible for overseeing the discharge of feudal obligations.

The Decision-Makers: A Coventry Story
The poem tells the story of Mark and Helen Mullins, an impoverished couple who lived outside Coventry and who were driven to a suicide pact by remorseless benefits sanctions and cuts to their income.

The Significs of Gentrification
Arbeitsscheu': German for 'workshy'.
Sunlight is the best disinfectant: phrase coined by American lawyer Louis Dembitz Brandeis.

Auld Reekie's Black Spot
Glaswegian playwright Paul Reekie committed suicide after his sickness benefits were abruptly withdrawn by the DWP in 2010.

Clapson's Cap
Incapacitated claimant and ex-soldier David Clapson died of a combination of near-starvation and diabetes complications due to having had his benefits cut by the DWP so that he could not afford to keep the electricity going to ensure his insulin remained at the correct temperature in his fridge; an appeal petition started by his sister Gill Thomson was successful in securing an independent enquiry into his death.
Spartacus Report: informal name given to the Responsible Reform Report by disabled people critiquing the government's efforts to slash their benefits and support has attracted huge attention.

Tan Raptures
Between 2011 and 2014, 91,740 incapacitated claimants died or committed suicide either while under assessment for Employment and Support Allowance (ESA) or after having had their ESA cut by the DWP after being declared *'fit for work'* by Atos (2,380 in a three year period). This poem was written prior to Work and Pensions Secretary Iain Duncan Smith's surprise resignation on 18th March 2016. The phrase *'Tan Raptures'* is a satirical euphemism implying some kind of perverse 'salvation' for the tens of thousands of claimant fatalities under Tory administration; it alludes to the brown or tan paper envelopes so dreaded by claimants, and to the biblical eschatological (*'last things'*) prophecy of *'the Rapture'*, when, at the time of the Second Coming, spirits of dead believers and those believers still living will be raised up into the sky to meet God.

First Rapture: *Disruptive Patterns*
Damascening: the art of inlaying different metals into one another.
Napoleon Hill: American author of *Think and Grow Rich* (1937).
Gabriel Tarde: a French social psychologist who came up with the theory of the herd mentality.

Second Rapture: *Compassion Fatigues*
Lictor: a Roman civil servant who was a bodyguard to magistrates who carried bundles of wooden rods and an axe bound together with ropes, tools for inflicting punishments on the guilty, called *fasces*, wherefrom the term fascism is thought to have derived.
Calum's List: a website by surviving relatives of those many claimant fatalities of the welfare cuts, including suicides, documented for public access (http://calumslist.org)

Third Rapture: *Eudemonia Ends in Damascene Moment*
Recumbentibus: a knockdown blow.
eudemonia: (Greek, 'eu' ('good') and 'daimōn' ('spirit')) concept of 'happiness', 'welfare', 'wellbeing', 'human flourishing', originating in Aristotlean ethics.

Fourth Rapture: *Something for Nothing*
Caxton House: offices of the DWP in Westminster.
Auguste Comte: (1798-1857), founder of sociology and positivism.
Tetragrammaton: the Hebrew word for God (theonym), once represented consonantally in the Latin letters *YHVH*, abbreviation for *Yahweh*.

Fifth Rapture: *Note on Alms*
Trussell: the Trussell Trust, primary provider of food banks.
The wolves/Which once infested our forests: from David Lloyd George's stirring speech as Liberal Chancellor during debates around the People's Budget of 1909/10.
Marcel Mauss: (1872-1950) French sociologist, nephew of Émile Durkheim.

Seventh Rapture: *Plantagenet Spring*
Atra mors: Latin for Black Death.

Eighth Rapture: *Kerygma & Seisaktheia*
Pact of the Catacombs: a pact, signed in 1965 near the end of the Second Vatican Council, containing 13 points regarding the relationship of the Roman Catholic clergy to the poor.
Kerygma: (Greek) preaching.
Weatherley: (Mike) Weatherley, former Tory MP for Hove who succcessfully campaigned to criminalise squatting under the Con-Dem Government.

Ninth Rapture: *Saints Gemma & Walter*
Gemma Galgani: (1878-1903), Italian mystic who is regarded as Patron Saint of students, pharmacists and the unemployed.

Tenth Rapture: *Brown Ominous*
isabelline: pale grey-yellow, fawn, cream or parchment colour.

Thirteenth Rapture: *Tan Rapture*
Entfremdung: (German) estrangement from *Gattungswesen* (*'species-essence'*), or more specifically in the Marxian sense, estrangement from one's own labour.

Fourteenth Rapture: *Two Types of Brown Envelopes*
Thoughtform: or Tulpa is the Tibetan concept of thoughts forming actual images, colours, shapes, forms, even actual sentient beings with personalities, which manifest outside of the human mind/head but are only perceptible to clairvoyants; a common meme of Theosophy.

Post-Rapture: *A Compromise Too Far*
Grayling (Chris) was employment minister under IDS during some of the worst administrative attacks on the unemployed and incapacitated. *Miller* (Maria) was the disability minister who oversaw the dismantling of the Remploy factory which employed disabled workers; *McVey* (Esther) was her equally unrepentant successor, both were responsible for overseeing Atos and Maximus WCAs.
Braunhemden: (German) *'brownshirt'*, uniform and nickname of the Nazi Storm Troopers.
haruspex: was a person in Ancient Rome trained to practice a form of divination called *haruspicy* (*haruspicina*) the inspection of the entrails of sacrificed animals.
Mr. Crabb: Stephen Crabb, successor to 'IDS' as Secretary of State for the DWP. This stanza contains several excerpts from Iain Duncan Smith's resignation letter of 18th March 2016.

Addendum: BENEDICTIONS
The names and details of these late victims of Tory *'welfare reform'* are taken from the Black Triangle Campaign website http://blacktrianglecampaign.org.

Acknowledgements

Some of these poems have previously appeared as different versions in: *The Communist Review; Culture Matters; Fit for Work – Poets Against Atos; The International Times; Militant Thistles; The Morning Star; Occupy Poetry; Poems for Freedom* (River Books); *Poet-in-Residence; Poetry and All That Jazz; Poetry & Poets in Rags; Red Poets.*